# CHALLENGING LATE CAPITALISM, NEO-LIBERAL GLOBALIZATION, AND MILITARISM:

# BUILDING A PROGRESSIVE MAJORITY

By Harry R. Targ
Purdue University

© Harry R. Targ
ISBN: 978-1-4116-7726-5
ChangeMaker Publications, Chicago 2006
3411 W Diversey, Suite 3, Chicago IL 60647
www.lulu.com/changemaker

*"I hate a song that makes you think that you are not any good. I hate a song that makes you think that you are just born to lose. Bound to lose. No good to nobody. No good for nothing. Because you are too old or too young or too fat or too slim. Too ugly or too this or too that. Songs that run you down or poke fun at you on account of your bad luck or hard traveling. I am out to fight those songs to my very last breath of air and my last drop of blood..."*

*Woody Guthrie*

*"Continued study and research into the origins of the folk music of various peoples in many parts of the world revealed that there is a world body-a universal body- of folk music based upon a universal pentatonic (five tone) scale. Interested as I am in the universality of (hu)mankind-in the fundamental relationship of all peoples to one another-this idea of a universal body of music intrigued me, and I pursued it along many fascinating paths."*

*Paul Robeson*

# *Acknowledgements*

*At the dawn of 2006, the people of the globe face crises of violence, poverty, and powerlessness. Massive movements of outrage and protest have emerged in response to the crises. However, common analyses of the underlying causes of the great pain and suffering of peoples everywhere and the appropriate forms of political mobilization and action to rectify the situations have been lacking. Even more, as the hopes and dreams of those who came before have been dashed, cynicism has replaced vision.*

*Progressives need to return to analysis and to envisioning humane alternative futures as we continue to fight against exploitation, racism, poverty, and war. This extended essay is designed to contribute to the analysis and debate: about global capitalism, about militarism, and about building progressive movements. It attempts to link scholarly rigor and commitment to change and to proposals for practical political work. It also seeks to participate in that great tradition of scholarship and activism that has played a modest but significant role in the social movements of the last many years.*

*If there is any value to the ideas and analyses that follow, they have resulted from profound influences. These include Bob Perrucci, Carolyn Perrucci, Dave Cormier, Berenice Carroll, Clint Fink, Kermit Scott, John McCartney, Fred Muskal, Peter Knauss, Jim Berlin, and many other students and friends who dropped an idea here, made a criticism there, that stuck with me.*

*In recent years, I have had the extraordinary opportunity to meet and work with political intellectuals and activists in the Committees of Correspondence for Democracy and Socialism who by their example demonstrate passion for people and lifetimes of commitment to building a better world: Charlene Mitchell, Pat Fry, Mark Solomon, Carl Bloice, Mildred Williamson, Carl Davidson, Todd Freeberg, and Ted Pearson among them.*

*Rebecca Targ makes it clear that ideals and commitments can be transferred from generation to generation, but at the same time that they reflect some of the old, they must be infused with the new. She is an inspiration as she "carries it on" in her own way.*

*My ideas, my commitments, my politics, my life work, would not have been possible without the solidarity, friendship, and love of Dena B. Targ. As a scholar activist in her own right, she has been instrumental in helping me try to be the same. And, if there is any clarity to the ideas that follow, it is due to her red pen.*

# TABLE OF CONTENTS

Chapter 1: The Problem

Chapter 2: Late Capitalism and the Relevance of Ideas to Understand It.

Chapter 3: Globalization, Neo-Liberalism and Workers

*(with David Cormier, Institute for Labor Studies and Research, West Virginia University).*

Chapter 4: Military Spending and Economic Crisis.

Chapter 5: Progressive Movements in the United States.

Chapter 6: Where Do We Go From Here?

# Chapter 1

## THE PROBLEM

*Hurricane Katrina or The Emperor Has No Clothes*

Late summer, 2005, Hurricane Katrina vaults through the Gulf states destroying property, blowing holes in the levee that kept New Orleans from drowning, and leaving hundreds of thousands of people homeless, trapped in a sea of water, and despair. The city of New Orleans is destroyed; at first estimate, forever. Towns and cities in Alabama and Mississippi hit by the Hurricane experience similar destruction although the press coverage of the plight of their residents receives less attention. Initial estimated numbers killed from the apocalypse total 10,000 people. While later figures are much lower, no full accounting is ever presented.

This greatest "natural" disaster in U.S. history uncovered ugly truths about American society. First, the vast majority of those victimized by the Hurricane were poor and Black people. They lived in parts of the cities and rural areas around the Gulf that were most vulnerable to winds and water. They were less likely to have the resources to prepare for the disaster or to protect themselves when it hit. Also, as the days that followed made crystal clear, resources to rescue them from harm's way were of little interest to government authorities.

Second, federal agencies, which had been the beneficiaries of billions of dollars to provide national security, freedom from acts of terrorism, physical infrastructure to protect against flooding and other natural disasters, and disaster relief had totally failed to mitigate the horrific brutality of Hurricane Katrina. Official spokespersons from the relevant agencies evidenced ignorance of what was actually occurring in the ravaged areas. The president of the United States even praised the work of some of the agency heads who lacked any evidence of competence or concern.

Third, the major emergency support force that historically is mobilized during periods of such disasters, the National Guard, was at less than full capacity because a third to one- half of the troops usually available were fighting a foreign war in Iraq to protect United States control of Middle East oil. Young men and women from Louisiana, Mississippi, and Alabama were in Iraq killing innocent victims instead of being in their home states rescuing the homeless.

Fourth, during the depths of the crisis of displaced persons seeking shelter, water, food, and clothing and as the desperate and the dead were viewed on television floating down the flooded streets of the city, oil companies were raising the price of gasoline at the pump by a third. *No mainstream politicians made any proposals to freeze the price of gasoline. The deaths and destruction wrought by Hurricane Katrina were used to transfer wealth from the working people of the United States to a handful of oil companies whose profit rates doubled and tripled.*

Finally, when the president launched a rescue program five days after the Hurricane hit the Gulf, he emphasized prayer, encouraged "faith-based" groups to raise money, endorsed the Red Cross as a major relief agency player, and with Congress only allocated modest funds for relief efforts.

Later, while more government money was being proposed, major corporations and oil companies pledged funds for rescue and recovery. Ironically, the same multinational corporations that created the grotesquely unequal distribution of wealth and income in the country committed themselves to modest relief efforts. As was suggested in an early post-Hurricane commentary by Michael Parenti, the depths of the pain and suffering from the natural disaster must be seen as intimately connected to the market economic model that would be trumpeted as the solution to the effects of the Hurricane.

So in the summer, 2005, it became clear to many Americans what they either did not see or chose to ignore; they live in a society deeply split between the wealthy and the poor, the white and people of color, the powerful and the powerless, and huge corporations and isolated individuals. Along with the long struggle to reconstruct lives in the Gulf Coast, the American people need to reflect on the real meaning of Katrina and to develop an understanding of the U.S. empire in all its nakedness. And as that understanding is occurring, masses of people of all backgrounds need to come together to build a popular movement to change the economic and political system that allows a natural disaster to have such devastating consequences for its victims.

## Another World is Possible

September, 2004, Hurricane Ivan hit the island nation of Cuba with 160 mile an hour winds. Over 1.5 million Cubans were evacuated from their homes. People traveled with family members, pets, some possessions, and neighborhood doctors who know the needs of their neighbors. No Cuban died.

A UN spokesperson praised Cuban hurricane procedures as a model for poor countries and even those more developed. In June of the following year, during Hurricane Dennis, Fidel Castro counseled his people to follow the evacuation plan and not worry about property damage. He said that the priority in the evacuation plan was protecting human life. Although 20 people died and 85 percent of the electrical grid was damaged during Hurricane Dennis, Cuban society was not brought to a halt. In both of these cases, no violence or looting occurred. In Cuba, benefits from the economic system are shared and pain and suffering is equally shared. Hurricanes are not experienced differently by class, race, or gender (United Nations; Taylor Martin).

## Human Misery: A Global Problem

A *New York Times* columnist (Brooks) proposed an apt metaphor relating natural disaster to sociological analysis. He suggested that sometimes horrific winds, rain, or shattering earthquakes brush away the superstructure of societies and uncover their underlying reality. Hurricanes Ivan, Dennis, and Katrina washed away mythologies about the United States and Cuba, leaving a clearer vision of the harsh realities of people's lives that its victims knew but others could not comprehend. In the examples above, the United States, for all its collective wealth and power, was seen by the world to be a society of gross inequalities in wealth, income, and opportunity. Most importantly, the world saw a government seemingly ill-equipped, either by choice or inadvertence, to respond to the needs of its poorest members. And, for those who cared to look, Cuba, a poor country, demonstrated its commitment to the basic survival needs of all its citizens.

Looking at the global economy, we see a grotesquely unequal distribution of wealth and income between countries and within them. A handful of billionaires have more wealth than 48 countries. Among the top 100 economic actors, in terms of accumulated capital, 52 are corporations and 48 are countries. About 200 multinational corporations produce one-third of all that is produced on the face of the globe (Anderson, Cavanagh, and Lee, 69).

At the bottom of the social and economic system, a little less than half the world's population lives on $2 a day; 1.7 billion live on less than $1 a day. Global inequality between countries and within them has increased over the last thirty years. Joblessness as a central element of poverty continues at alarming rates all across the globe. And to compound the problem of unequal wealth, income, and survival, growing strains on the environment further reduce people's capacities to sustain life.

Even the United States, the "last remaining superpower" after the Cold War, has pockets of poverty and human suffering comparable to the poorest of countries. Infant mortality rates have risen over the last five years. The number of individuals, families, and children living in poverty has increased. Comprehensive health care is limited to those with higher incomes. And for most Americans, real wages today are lower than they were in the 1990s or the 1970s. The world of the 21st century is one of incredible scientific and technological development-in communication, transportation, production, exploration, and biological advance. And, in contradistinction, the world of the twenty-first century is one of incredible human misery-hunger, ill-health, lack of housing and access to basic resources such as water, and income. How could such human misery exist in this world of development, wealth, and power?

The pages that follow address this question, drawing upon relevant Marxist theory as a guide, and suggest ways in which capitalism has contributed both to the development and the underdevelopment of human existence. Throughout the text, and particularly at its end, I discuss issues of social change and growing popular resistance. One of the central themes of human history is that rising inequality in wealth, power, and human suffering creates its opposite, organized resistance to its perpetuation. A renaissance in that resistance has been visible all across the world for a decade. The question for concerned citizens of the world is how to nurture and support it effectively and how to be actively engaged in the construction of a better world.

*Bibliography*

Anderson, Sarah, John Cavanagh, and Thea Lee. *Field Guide to the Global Economy,* New Press, 2005.

Brooks, David. "The Storm After the Storm," *The New York Times*, September 1, 2005.

Parenti, Michael. "How the Free Market Killed New Orleans," at www.zmag.org/sustainers/content/2005_09/03parenti.cfm

Taylor Martin, Susan. "Cuba offers Model of How to Plan for Disasters," *St. Petersburg Times*, September 9, 2005, at www.ocregister.com/ocz/2005/09/05/sectionsnews/news/article_6684 73.php

United Nations. "Cuba: A Model in Hurricane Risk Management," www. UN.org/news/press/docs.2004/iha 943.doc.htm, 14/09/2004

# Chapter 2

LATE CAPITALISM AND THE RELEVANCE
OF MARXIST IDEAS FOR UNDERSTANDING IT

*Introduction*

Over the last 25 years enormous changes have occurred in the global economy and in national economies. Capitalism, which seemed on the verge of destruction during the oil crises and economic stagnation of the 1970s, recovered and extended its tentacles all across the globe, particularly as a result of the collapse of Socialist regimes in Europe and Asia. During this time, the negative consequences of capitalism generated massive mobilizations of workers, women, indigenous peoples, and youth. However, capitalist institutions and armed states have been able to repress and defuse revolutionary ferment while extending neo-liberal economic policies everywhere.

Marx argued that the material advances in capitalism-economic, scientific, and technological-were historically unique as were the levels of misery, marginalization, alienation, and victimization stimulated by them. The rise of capitalism stimulated increased resistance to it; sometimes organized and effective. But, when the Cold War ended, traditional movements opposed to capitalism's advance became confused, fragmented, and ineffective. Without the anchor of a Socialist Bloc or revolutionary regimes or an ideologically and institutionally coherent mass-based Socialist movement the organized Left began to disintegrate into a broad array of separate issue-oriented groups. By the late 1990s, however, massive and increasingly organized opposition to war, neo-liberal globalization, racism, sexism, and homophobia began to spread throughout the world. Despite this new resistance to the byproducts of global capitalism an ideologically coherent anti-capitalist movement remains to be constructed.

Historically the Marxist tradition has provided an analysis and rigorous understanding of the capitalist system and has supplied theoretical tools for practical political work. Therefore, it is critical to develop a Marxist theoretical and historical analysis for our time. What is the nature of the capitalist mode of production today? How is it different from what capitalism has historically been? What remains the same today as was originally analyzed by Marx and his followers? What contradictions are embedded in the capitalist mode of production? How does an understanding of capitalism as an economic system relate to politics and political struggle?

With so much pain and suffering experienced all around us, it is of vital importance to address these questions and to test out the answers that emerge in practical political work. The materials below respond to a variety of questions about theory, about capitalism, about politics, and about political practice.

*What Remains Relevant in Marxist Theory?*

Marx grasped the underlying structures and dynamics of the capitalist mode of production, the contradictions within it, and the possibilities for struggling against its most negative features. Several of his central hypotheses, still relevant today, are discussed below.

*First,* the capitalist system is built on the exploitation of the working class. Those who own or control the means of production buy the labor power of the dispossessed, extracting the value of the goods and services produced by them. In short, value derives from human labor power and it is appropriated by capitalists. Workers, whether manufacturing or service, intellectual or manual, produce all wealth.

*Second,* because capitalists and workers struggle for control of the value of the goods and services produced by workers, class struggle is embedded in the economic system. Exploitation is not primarily about the extraction of some excessive amount of labor by unusually greedy and immoral capitalists. Rather exploitation is intrinsic to the system. All existing societies were based on the division between those who owned or controlled property and those who did not. Therefore struggle between the rich and powerful and the poor is intrinsic to class society. Class conflict is nowhere greater than in capitalist societies.

*Third,* capitalism is a class system in which the economic ruling class gains more of the value of the product of labor than workers. Consequently, the entire system generates inequality. Often in history this inequality in distribution of value has led to expanding misery of the majority of citizens.

*Fourth,* in a capitalist system, each capitalist is compelled by the competitive nature of the economic system to accumulate more capital. Capitalists expand their profits and accumulate more capital or their enterprises are taken over by their competitors.

*Fifth,* capitalism breeds cutthroat competition. Some capitalists accumulate more capital while others are forced from participation in the system. Therefore, the general tendency of capitalist competition historically has been a qualitative shift from huge numbers of small economic units (central to the utopian "invisible hand" of Adam Smith) to increasing concentrations of capital. As economic historian Douglas Dowd put it, capitalism's two fundamental dynamics are exploitation (as described above) and expansion.

Expansion refers both to concentration of economic power in smaller numbers of hands and the spread of economic power over greater geographic areas. Lenin analyzed the historic evolution of capitalism from its industrial phase to its monopoly phase. He suggested that expansion led to colonies and neo-colonies. (In our own day capitalism has led to "globalization.") He added that expansion has also meant increasing control of economic sectors, then the overall economy, by a small number of multinational corporations and international banks. For him, imperialism was the monopoly stage of capitalism.

*Sixth,* the ownership class accumulates more and more wealth and, therefore, typically that class also accumulates enormous political power. The state usually represents the interests of the ruling class but because of a variety of conditions or specific historical contexts, the state often has become contested terrain; that is, workers and their allies exercise significant influence over governmental policy.

*Seventh,* the capital accumulation process leads capitalists to traverse the globe in pursuit of investment opportunities, cheap labor, and customers for goods produced in the core countries or in poorer countries, and vital natural resources, such as oil and water. Overseas expansion by rich countries in support of their manufacturing and financial capitalists, has stimulated the "globalization of capital" driven by, among other reasons, a tendency for the rates of profit to fall and for capitalism to overproduce goods and services that remain under-consumed within the country of origin.

*Eighth,* of all the contradictions intrinsic to capitalism, the starkest is the historically evolving misery of the masses. This is the general law of capitalism.

*Finally,* Marxism provides a method for understanding the capitalist system, uncovering its mystifications, and engaging in practical political activity to reform or overthrow it. The methodology is historical, materialist, and dialectical.

Marx counsels scholar/activists to seek to understand the world in its historical context. The present is intimately tied to the past as the future is tied to the present. Theoretical insights are "tested" in concrete historical circumstances. In reconstructing the past, the historian analyzes the political practice of a given time in terms of the context in which the political activity occurred.

Marx insists that there is a fundamental connection between the production and reproduction of life, the organization of work, the distribution of wealth and power, and the way people live, think, and act. Material conditions, primarily economics, frame politics, society, and culture.

In addition, Marx claimed that the world is contradictory. The flowering new capitalism of his day was creating its own gravediggers, workers. This economic machine had embedded within it the seeds of both growth and destruction. All of life, even the human physiology of growth, is also movement toward death.

Political analysts and political activists, therefore, must understand contradictions in the real lived circumstances in which they are working. Concretely, activists should remember that situations or political forces are neither all one thing nor another, all good or all bad. And in our own day, the miseries of global capitalism are generating the resistance and the visions of an alternative way of living that can transform it.

*Features of Late Capitalism*

The Belgian economist Ernest Mandel introduced the concept "late capitalism" in writings on the economy in the 1970s. The Marxist literary scholar Fredric Jameson borrowed the term to sub-title his book, *Postmodernism, or the Cultural Logic of Late Capitalism* (1991). These authors claimed that capitalism had qualitatively changed from the capitalist mode of production described by Lenin as "monopoly capitalism." They theorized about the changing character of capitalist production-what is produced, by whom, with what technologies, and how the products are distributed. Also, they claimed that the globalization, financial speculation, and automation of the new capitalism had transformed what we typically call culture- what we see, read, hear, consume, and believe.

The concept "late capitalism" is useful because it suggests something about this time in capitalism's development historically; that capitalism may be overdeveloped and hence subject to stresses, strains, and pressures for radical change; that capitalism today is characterized by a variety of new features requiring analysis; and that among these features are special kinds of economic concentration, globalization, and cultural homogenization.

Informed by basic insights from the Marxist tradition, theorists of "late capitalism," which today include numerous writers on global capitalism, identify major features of the contemporary political economy of capitalism.

*First,* capitalism, by any kind of measure, has become more concentrated than ever before in world history and the concentration has been particularly marked in the financial sector and in manufacturing. For example, Anderson and Cavanagh *(Multinational Monitor)* reported in 1996 that the top 200 corporations had combined sales exceeding the value of the Gross National Products, the value of all the goods and services produced in a country, of all but the nine wealthiest nations. By 2002, the sales of the top 200 corporations equaled 28 percent of the world's GDP. In 2003, 52 of the top 100 economic actors in the world were corporations while 48 were nations. Wal-Mart was the nineteenth largest world economic actor, just below Belgium and ahead of Sweden. As Anderson, Cavanaugh, and Lee put it, "the largest 200 firms are the dominant engines of the global economy" (68). As to country of origin, *Business Week* (July, 1998) presented data on the "global 1000" corporations. U.S. based corporations accounted for 480 of the 1,000, with European companies totaling 350.

Several commentators point out that concentration in the financial sector constitutes what is really new about the era of globalization. Transnational banks and investment firms promote financial speculation, facilitate trade and investment between countries, loan money to nations in debt, and buy and sell stocks, bonds, and currencies. It is estimated that $1.5 trillion is exchanged every day thus creating a "virtual" or "casino" economy exceeding the "real" economy of trade in goods and services. One economist estimated that in the 1970s over 90 percent of the value of all cross-national transactions involved trade in goods and services but by the 1990s over 90 percent of transactions involved the buying and selling of stocks, bonds, and currencies (Litaer).

In 1999 the assets of the twenty largest transnational banks exceeded $425 trillion (Kegley and Wittkopf, 227). Sixteen of them accounted for more than 60 percent of speculation in foreign exchange markets that year. As Greider and others point out, financial speculation has been responsible for the severe economic crises that have occurred in recent years, such as the Asian financial crisis.

The consolidation of economic power, in manufacturing, service, and finance distinguishes the last 25 years from the prior 100 years. Functional activities of the new super-corporations also have changed. Of the sales of the top 200 multinational corporations in recent years, half were in just five economic sectors: trading and banking (financial), automobiles and electronics (manufacturing), and retailing. Henwood reported that in 1991 finance, insurance, and real estate (FIRE) surpassed the manufacturing contribution to the US GDP for the first time. By 1996, the non-manufacturing sectors of the economy accounted for $1.4 trillion in output while manufacturing totaled $1.3 trillion. Profits and sales derived from FIRE accounted for less than 20 percent of gross investment in 1950 and over 40 percent by 1990. On a worldwide basis, 42 percent of the world's stocks were held by U.S. financial corporations in 1996 (Henwood, 1998).

*Second*, there have been significant changes in capitalist relations of production and distribution over the last thirty years from what some theorists refer to as "Fordism" to "Post-Fordism." Fordism refers to a system of production and distribution in which the working class engages in the production of the largest quantity of commodities possible using the latest assembly line techniques for distribution to as large a market of consumers as possible. And, since the workers themselves constitute the core consumers of the products produced, the Fordist system assumed, workers must be paid a wage sufficient to purchase the goods. In other words, the capitalist system that developed out of the industrial revolution of the nineteenth century and expanded in the twentieth century was based on high mass production and high mass consumption. Sectors of the working class were paid a wage and received workplace benefits so that they could afford to purchase the goods they were producing. The system was called "Fordism" because Henry Ford believed he needed to provide a sufficient wage for the workers he hired to build the Model T automobile to purchase the cars they were producing.

The Great Depression led to massive unemployment (25 percent of the work force). Economists influenced by John Maynard Keynes recommended that more money needed to be transferred to workers via state programs to stimulate demand and create economic recovery. This logic was central to New Deal programs in the United States and emerging social democracies in Europe both before and after World War II. Some capital was transferred to workers as government programs, or substitutes for wages, so that they could purchase goods to fuel an economic recovery.

The Fordist system was based on high mass production and high mass consumption. Post-Fordism refers to a system of capitalist production that prioritizes a higher, and smaller, income segment of the population for consumption of goods. Products, including raw materials, capital goods, commodities for sale, are produced in just enough quantity for a carefully targeted population. "Just-in-time" production replaces mass production. Goods are produced based on specific estimates of the number of products that will be sold. Shopping malls and gentrified urban neighborhoods are the sites for targeting wealthier consumers. The decline in higher paying manufacturing jobs reduces the pool of workers who can consume the goods produced. The Post-Fordist system is based on super-exploitation of workers, often in overseas sweatshops, and the sale of higher priced goods and services to smaller sectors of the population with higher incomes than the traditional working class.

Obviously, the process of targeting smaller higher income sectors of the working population for consumption has not eliminated consumption by the working poor and unemployed. All people are enticed to purchase allegedly cheaper goods from retailers such as Wal-Mart. But increasingly consumerism is based upon incurring debt. Consumer debt drives the Post-Fordist economy.

During the 1990s, total consumer debt for the first time exceeded total income in the United States. Growing personal debt has gone up as government transfer payments to poor and working people have declined. But, despite qualitative increases in indebtedness, workers have trouble affording the goods produced. Reduced demand for goods and services has led to reduced rates of profit from manufacturing. To overcome declining rates of profit labor costs are reduced by moving manufacturing to low wage poor countries. In addition multinational corporations shift from investing in further manufacturing to financial speculation. In the end, the loss of high paying manufacturing jobs has been a significant byproduct of the Post-Fordist transformation of the relations of production.

The shift from Fordism to Post-Fordism is a tendency; a tendency that will make sizeable and growing percentages of the working populations, of core capitalist states as well as poor states, become obsolete as wage earners and consumers. Survival of inner city youth, people of color and the aged in the United States to masses of people in Africa and Latin America requires inventing ways to secure basic sustenance. So-called informal sector activities become the means by which growing numbers of people (40 percent of working age Latin Americans) avoid starvation. The shift from Fordism to Post-Fordism mirrors the shift in global capitalism from manufacturing to service, the movement of manufacturing capital to poor countries where workers work for less, the rise of the informal sector, and growing joblessness and income and wealth inequality around the world.

*Third,* with the growing concentration of capital (in the United States and in the global economy), the surging importance of financial (speculative) capital, the shift from Fordism to post-Fordism and increasingly marginalized informal sector struggles for survival, there has occurred a growing inequality in the distribution of wealth and income. Gaps in wealth and income have been increasing for some thirty years in the United States, and in the world at large.

Chart 1 derived from 2001 data presented by Doug Henwood (2003) illustrates the magnitude of the gaps between rich and poor in the United States:

## Chart 1: Distribution of Income and
## Wealth in the United States, 2001

|            | Bottom 90% | Top 10% | Top 1% |
|------------|------------|---------|--------|
| Income     | 61         | 39      | 14.5   |
| Net Worth  | 31.2       | 69.9    | 32.7   |
| Assets     | 35.5       | 64.6    | 29.5   |
| Stocks     | 11.9       | 88.1    | 52.9   |
| Bonds      | 4.2        | 95.8    | 64.4   |
| Debts      | 73.8       | 26.1    | 5.9    |

While the top ten percent of the income earners received "only" 39 percent of the nation's income, it controlled 64.6 percent of its assets, 88.1 percent of its stock, 95.8 percent of its bonds, and had only 26.1 percent of its debt.

The Economic Policy Institute reported that since 1983 the top one percent of wealth holders had 30-40 percent of the country's wealth and the bottom 80 percent held only 16 percent, and for the last 40 years 80 percent of all wealth in American has been held by the top 20 percent of households (Mishel, Bernstein, and Boushey, 2003, 281). In 1979, the income of the top one percent was 33 times greater than the bottom 20 percent. By 1997, the top one percent had 88.5 times more income than the bottom 20 percent (73).

Persistent and growing economic inequality has been noted around the globe as well. (Data below and in Chapter 3 illustrate this). The United Nations Development Program, which issues reports on global development and underdevelopment, reported in the late

1990s that gaps between rich and poor countries and within rich and poor countries had grown over the last several years and that at least one quarter of the world's population lived in poverty. A 2003 UNDP report indicated that 54 countries were worse off economically than they had been ten years earlier. Earlier reports suggested that less than 400 billionaires had combined assets greater than annual incomes of countries with populations totaling 45 percent of the world's population (Rowan).

A 2005 UN reported called "The World Social Situation: The Inequality Predicament," indicated that the gaps between rich and poor peoples and countries had grown over the decade since the Summit for Social Development in 1995. The report noted that 80 percent of the world's Gross Domestic Product was controlled by one billion people while 20 percent was shared by five billion people. Nearly one quarter of working people in the world earned less than $1 a day, the World Bank standard for extreme poverty. Nearly 3 billion people lived on less than $2 a day. Global poverty, the report claimed, was related to inequalities in literacy, health, jobs, as well as to violence.

*Fourth*, despite modest improvements from time to time the general living conditions of workers in the U.S. have been eroding. Wages, working conditions, job security, hours of work, and numbers of those living in poverty were worse in the mid-1990s than the 1970s, and despite a short-term increase in wages in the late 1990s, the American worker in the new century was not as well off as his counterpart of thirty years earlier. For example, the percentage of the work force that earned at or below official poverty levels grew from 23.5 percent in 1973 to 28.6 percent in 1997. The percentage of Black workers earning poverty wages increased from 36.8 percent to 38.2 percent in those years, and Hispanic workers from 34.3 percent to 46.7 percent. Male workers who had less than a high school education, a high school diploma, some college or a college degree all earned less in real dollars in 1997 than they did in 1973. For women, those with a college degree earned more in 1995 than in 1973 but the trajectory of real earnings was down for those other women workers with some or no college (Michel, Bernstein and Schmitt, 1999, 136-142).

During the second Clinton administration, the percent of workers earning poverty level wages declined, but by 2003 the trend was reversed. The percentage of those earning poverty level wages had gone up. Furthermore, unemployment was two percentage points higher, 3.2 private sector jobs had been lost, and real family income had declined in 2001 and 2002 (Mishel, November 3, 2003).

The editors of *Monthly Review* (April, 2003) addressed the recent impacts of the capitalist economy on U.S. workers. Over 2 million jobs were lost between 2001 and 2003. Eighty-seven percent of job losses became permanent (up from 50 percent in prior recessions). Layoffs of those who did eventually return to work were for longer periods than in the past. Real unemployment rates, including discouraged workers and involuntary part-time workers, were double the official rates. By any measure of unemployment, African American women and men experienced twice the loss of whites while Hispanic unemployment rates were 25 percent greater than those of whites. African-American and other minority youth experience up to five times greater unemployment than whites over age 25.

Additional indicators reflected the stresses of the economy on people's lives. Demands for emergency food assistance, shelter, and welfare rose as government programs were slashed. The Center on Budget and Policy priorities estimated that states experienced almost $160 billion in budget deficits between 2001 and 2003 which led to radical shortfalls in health care and resources for public education, public safety, child care, and disaster relief in 2005.

Exacerbating growing inequalities and declining living conditions, the Bush administration successfully lobbied for massive tax cuts for the rich which shifted more wealth and income from the many to the few. In addition, the president lobbied for radical reductions in all governmental services and the transfer of programs formerly residing in the federal government to budget strapped states. Every effort was made to privatize all public services-from education to social security to welfare. The twenty-first century U.S. economy experienced    stagnation,    declining    real    wages,    and    high unemployment, coupled with bloated military expenditures. Every public program, except the military, was being downsized. In 2005, economic and social disaster was confounded by hurricane disaster.

*Fifth*, in the United States, the vast majority of the population, largely the working class has been marginalized, "deskilled", and fragmented. On the one hand, the nature of work has been transformed over the last 100 years to increase management control of every phase of the work process. As Braverman suggested in the 1970s, much of the conceptual organization of work and control over decisions about worker behavior had been continued to be transferred from the shop floor to the CEO's office. Braverman said that with applications of post-Taylorist worker control techniques, the work force was steadily being reduced to simple bodily motions. His/her work was "deskilled;" that is, the work was reduced to the simplest of physical and mental behaviors. Management had expropriated the power that came with knowledge of the job. As the twentieth century evolved, entrepreneurial and craft skills were destroyed and workers were transformed into deskilled factory and then service workers. Loss of power and control manifested in work skills and the homogenizing of all work activity meant that more and more of the working population had become proletarianized.

Proletarianization meant that more and more workers activities were reduced to simple motions under management control. One kind of worker was fundamentally similar to every other kind of worker. Workers had become powerless and marginalized in the capitalist system; a mass of homogenized bodies and minds.

It is critical to be aware of the fragmentation of workers as well. For example, the traditional industrial working class now constitutes less than twenty percent of the work force. The largest share of the work force today is in the service sector, from banking, to insurance, to health care, to fast food. An increasing share of workers is acquiring computer skills and according to some, for example Robert Reich, educating workers to become "symbolic analysts" is necessary to overcome structural unemployment and declining real wages. Fragmentation in the end refers to the differentiation of work into numerous discrete activities and managerial control. Computerization has advanced the process.

In addition, a significant share of the work force is contingent and/or made up of part-time employees. Manpower Incorporated, a personnel service that places temporary workers has been among the largest employers in the United States. Temps are often hired for factory jobs earning half the wages of their co-workers without any health and pension benefits. Ironically, temps sometimes train other temps or full-time replacements. Finally, the modern working class includes a significant percentage of working age men and women who are unable to gain jobs and who have to survive in the underground economy.

Fragmentation of the work force, as with proletarianization, is the result of the changing means and relations of production, The introduction of technology, just-in-time production schemes, downsizing and shifting production overseas, Post-Fordist policies, transforming work, the shift from production to service, and decentralizing production facilities and service outlets all materially have refashioned the relations of production. In addition, fragmentation of the working class in late capitalism is reinforced by the perpetuation and use of racism, sexism, and homophobia by capital. Lack of access to jobs and pay equity, and under-representation in labor unions, attacks on affirmative action, and raising the "threat of immigration," all effectively drive a wedge between sectors of a working class that is already divided by virtue of changes in the means of production. In other words, the world of the worker in the United States and globally is one of marginalization, proletarianization, and fragmentation.

*Contradictions in the Political Economy of Capitalism Today*

As suggested at the outset, Marx advanced a method for understanding and acting on the world that was historical, materialist, and dialectical. A central element of this method was the use of the idea of "contradiction." In simple terms it suggested to analysts that they look for the seeds of opposing tendencies and phenomena embedded in social processes; that no social process, development, or institution could be characterized as either one thing or another. The world of social and political relations was a complex world and analysis and political activity required the subtle reading that exploring contradictions required. It is argued here that contradictions of the political economy of late capitalism bear upon progressive politics

*First*, the concentration of capital has reached levels unparalleled in human history. This means smaller numbers of corporations and banks control more and more of economic relations within countries and between them. However, this concentration of capital has accelerated competition between these corporations and banks such that the struggle for survival of parts of the global political economy, and the entire capitalist political economy, is more desperate as the years pass. This means that corporations and banks are in competition with each other and capitalist states are in competition with each other even as the biggest economic actors consolidate their economic control across borders.

For example, the movement toward "free trade" is supposed to create one global economy embodied in the World Trade Organization. However, this vision of a global trading network has stimulated the creation of regional trade regimes such as the North America Free Trade Agreement (NAFTA), the European Union, and the Asian Pacific Economic Cooperation organization. In the long run regional trade might increase competition and conflict between the United States in the Western Hemisphere, Europe, and Asia.

Within the United States, economic concentration is reflected in the declining numbers of individuals and corporations that control more and more of the wealth of the country. Competition among huge corporations exists even though the rule of capital is hegemonic. Competition and disintegration is reflected also in struggles among those capitalist organizations whose interests are global in competition economically and politically with capitalist organizations that derive their profits from largely internal sources (real estate interests, energy corporations, retail trade, and service corporations).

*Second*, late capitalism is characterized by extraordinary scientific and technological achievements. From instantaneous communication, to the computerization of production, to the production of products using skills of workers from several countries simultaneously, to transplant surgeries, to genetic engineering, humans have the capacity to eliminate onerous and dangerous physical labor, reduce the incidence of disease, cure heretofore deadly diseases, feed the world, and empower people politically and culturally. And, by virtue of global media, the world's citizens are aware of these human potentials. However, the reality is that the new technology, the new "globalization," has created the opposite, human misery. Marx's general law of capitalism seems as true today as in his day and many more people are aware of the differences between human possibilities and realities now.

*Third,* late capitalism has ushered in significant increases in worker productivity so that a smaller percentage of workers who dig coal, make steel, build automobiles, or cut meat now produce significantly greater quantities of these goods. In macro-economic terms the percentage of higher wage industrial workers within the United States has declined and been replaced by lower paid service workers. Globally, significant shares of industrial production have been shifted from high paying work forces in core capitalist countries to very low paying work forces in poorer countries. The paradox of increased worker productivity, coupled with declining high paying jobs and income, is that more goods are being produced globally than can be consumed. This creates the classic contradiction of capitalist economics reflected in overproduction and under-consumption.

Further, the growing contradiction of over-production and under-consumption parallels and reinforces declining rates of profit, a tendency experienced by U.S. industrial capital from the 1960s to the 1980s. With declining profit rates, capital investment shifted from production to finance, including stocks, bonds, and currency speculation. President Nixon's withdrawal from the currency regulations of the Bretton Woods system and, later, President Reagan's tax cuts for the rich also benefited the shift from investments in goods and services to speculation. In general, global capitalism has shifted its priorities from producing consumable goods and services to electronic buying and selling. Meanwhile, the gaps between rich and poor grow, conquerable diseases spread, and human misery expands. The neo-liberal agenda forces countries to downsize their governments to attract foreign investors in industrial development at a time when such investors become more and more scarce.

However, even when foreign investors channel capital into poor countries, they precipitously shift their investments at the first hint of economic crisis. This was visibly reflected in the deep economic crisis of 1997 that destabilized East Asian "miracle" economies. In sum, with overproduction, under-consumption, financial speculation, and indebtedness at the heart of the system of neo-liberal globalization the entire global economy during the current era is "skating on thin ice."

*Fourth*, a significant feature of late capitalism is a qualitative increase in the ability to communicate across long distances and instantaneously. World citizens have the capacity, as never before, to acquire information about politics, cultures, science, and human experience. This technological wizardly has the potential to liberate humankind from provincialism, to facilitate the transmission of cultural contributions to the storehouse of wisdom, to educate the young, and to increase democratic participation in political systems. However, the new technology has meant the destruction of cultures, the homogenization of human experience, and the concentration of communications institutions such that twenty or so media groups produce about half of what the world reads, sees, hears, and probably believes about economics, politics, and culture. Some writers, such as Benjamin Barber, argue that the only resistance now to the full McDonaldization of the globe comes from religious fundamentalisms; that there is a profound need for social movements to seize control and democratize the means of cultural production.

*Fifth*, a fundamental contradiction of late capitalism is reflected in the character of the working class. On the one hand, as suggested above, that class everywhere is more homogenized, deskilled, and proletarianized than ever before. Braverman estimated in the 1970s that about 85 percent of U.S. working age people could realistically be categorized as working class whereas a century earlier the vast majority of those working were farmers. Today, by virtue of wages and income, job and economic insecurity, unhealthy conditions of work including speed-up and longer work hours, people employed share more in common in Detroit, Tucson, Juarez, Johannesburg, and Beijing than ever before.

On the other hand, the working class is more fragmented than at any time in the history of capitalism. This fragmentation includes job categories including production or service work, various job tenures including full or part-time, and unionized or non-union work sites. Most importantly, workers are divided by race, gender, sexual orientation, age, country of birth, and immigration status ("legal" or "illegal"). The material fragmentation is reinforced often by ideological fragmentation: anti-communism, identification with right-wing groups including militias and Christian fundamentalists, and single issue groups that organize around guns or against women's right to choose. Also large sectors of the working class still see their futures tied to the electoral victories of the Democratic Party yet remain overwhelmingly alienated from the political process.

*Challenges to Progressive Politics in the Era of Late Capitalism*

This portrait of late capitalism suggests several contradictions: the concentration of capital and intensifying conflict between sectors of capital; advancing science and technology and rising human misery; overproduction and under-consumption; monopoly control of a globalizing cultural apparatus and religious/cultural resistance to it; and an homogenization and fragmentation of the working class. These features suggest that global capitalism is integrating and disintegrating at the same time. For example:

-Global capitalism is increasingly dominated by a few hundred banks and corporations in a handful of countries and a few international financial organizations while the wealthy countries, dominant corporations and banks, and even the leading international financial organizations, the International Monetary Fund (IMF) and World Bank, engage in growing economic and political competition.

-Political forces in the United States representing international capital contest public policies with sectors of capital that represent domestic economic interests.

-Politics in core capitalist states involves intensifying competition between ruling class fractions who see the need for the state to defuse growing working class anger by adjusting social safety nets versus those conservative sectors of the ruling class who seek to dismantle all state funded economic programs.

-Conflict over state economic policies stimulates class fractions to appeal to different constituents among the marginalized. Thus, culture wars emerge as ruling class fractions appeal to more "liberal" or more "conservative" sectors of the majority populations of the country. Out of this maelstrom comes religious fundamentalism, single issue political struggles-such as anti-abortion and pro-gun campaigns and a politics centered around so-called "family values."

-Conflicts in international relations among powerful states, mostly capitalist, emerge over how the international system should be controlled. The United States has moved to establish a post-Cold War military hegemony ("the last remaining superpower") which has generated conflict with other nations over issues ranging from the war on Iraq, to land mines, to global warming, to the Cuban embargo, to trade preferences.

Metaphors of centrifugal and centripetal forces, accommodation and resistance, cooperation and conflict, and consolidation and disintegration apply very well to political economy in the era of late capitalism. In fact, the forces tearing apart capitalism are as intense as ever before. The vivid metaphors of growth and decay that were so dramatically expressed in *The Communist Manifesto* can help in understanding the contradictions of contemporary capitalism and the possibilities of radical social change everywhere.

Paradoxically, the working class is as fettered with the forces of disintegration, disarray, and conflict, as is late capitalism. One need only list elements of the fragmentation of the working people of the planet to understand the difficulties progressives face in building mass movements for fundamental change.

-Racism, the most divisive force in the history of the United States, remains virulent. Powerful politicians can talk about using abortion to reduce the numbers of Black babies, which, in the long run, would reduce the crime rate. On a global level, the United States can bomb people of color and make war on them with impunity and large percentages of the citizenry endorse and support the actions (at least for a time).

-Sexism remains institutionalized in work, in politics, in personal relationships, and in culture. Gains for women in public institutions have largely been made on capitalism's own terms so that popular culture celebrates the few women who break through the "glass ceiling." At the same time, the instruments of mass culture and education trumpet the virtues of the nuclear family, "stay-at-home moms," images of women still as primary care-givers for children, male partners, and the aged and poor. Meanwhile, working class women, particularly women of color, bear the heaviest burdens of the capitalist system and receive the least support from it. And, in the political arena, women's issues are marginalized rather than seen as part of the politics of the working class as a whole.

-Homophobia has become a major source of divisiveness among working people as gays and lesbians have asserted their rights to sexual preference and personal and political freedom. Right-wing politicians use issues such as gay marriage as lighting rods to divide the electorate. And paradoxically, movements struggling against homophobia sometimes conceive of their activities separate from or instead of struggles for Socialism and the liberation of all working people. Consequently, sectors of the gay and lesbian movement and also African-American and women's movements mobilize around identity issues to the exclusion of class issues. This occurs while those movements that are characterized more by class perspectives consciously choose to side-step identity issues, or, even worse, reject the concerns for racism, sexism, and homophobia.

-The politics of social and economic transformation-as reflected in the Socialist and communist movements of the early 1900s and the 1930s and the New Left of the 1960s-has been replaced by the politics of single issues. Progressives organize in groups around anti-war, nuclear, environmental, Central American, anti-IMF, living wage, and other single issues. Usually, such groups do not contextualize their issue mobilizations

in broader class, anti-racism, and anti-sexism perspectives and more generally the struggle for Socialism. Mass movements have become fragmented into a thousand different issue domains.

-The rightwing sectors of the economic ruling class have utilized the politics of the single issue to mobilize around so-called "culture wars" issues-against abortion, against-gun control, for school vouchers, against pornography- such that working people are drawn into emotionally charged campaigns that separate them from their brothers and sisters and thus fragment the working class. In many parts of the United States, working people vote for candidates on the basis of their stand on guns even as economic inequality, job loss, and declining income make their personal lives more painful. Nationally, working people are fragmented by differences in geography, economic context, local political culture, and political possibilities. Struggles around "free trade," living wage campaigns, immigration, vary by state and region.

-Finally, the left, broadly defined, disintegrated over the last twenty years, particularly after the collapse of Socialism. Traditional left parties deconstructed. Left intellectuals embraced various kinds of "post-Marxist," "post-modernist,"or "post-colonial" formulations of the contemporary crisis. Some progressives rejected all of their history after the collapse of the Soviet Union. They called for a totally new beginning; in short they rejected history and theoretical traditions. Others embraced new theoretical formulations, such as some variant of the "globalization" thesis that demands "new age" thinking. Finally, many progressive intellectuals rejected the older organic connection between intellectuals and the working class.

In sum, late capitalism is an era in the development of the mode of production in which growth and decay, assimilation and disintegration, consolidation of economic and political power and growing conflicts among its parts all are magnified. In terms of the relations of production, workers are more homogenized, deskilled, and controlled while they are fragmented in terms of jobs and job security, unionization, race, gender, sexual orientation, geography, ideology, culture, and politics. The challenge for 21st century progressives is to understand the decay of late capitalism and the opportunities it provides for social change and to develop strategies to overcome the fragmentation of the global working class.

*Bibliography*

Anderson, Sarah and John Cavanagh. "Corporate Empires," *Multinational Monitor*, December, 1996, http://multinationalmonitor/org/hyper/min 1296.00.html

Anderson, Sarah, John Cavanagh, and Thea Lee. *Field Guide to the Global Economy,* The New Press, 2005.

Barber, Benjamin. *Jihad Vs. McWorld*, 1996.

Braverman, Harry. *Labor and Monopoly Capital*, Monthly Review, 1973.

*Business Week*. July, 1998.

Center on Budget and Policy Priorities. "A Brief Update on State Fiscal Conditions and the Effects of Federal Policies on State Budgets," September 13, 2004, www.cbpp.org/9-13-04 sfp.htm

Dowd, Douglas. *U.S. Capitalist Development Since 1976. Of, By, and for Which People*. M.E. Sharpe, 1993.

Greider, William. *One World Ready or Not*, Simon and Schuster, 1997.

Henwood, Doug. *After the New Economy*, The New Press, 2003, 123.

Henwood, Doug. *Wall Street*. Verso, 1998, 56-117.

Jameson, Fredric. *Postmodernism or the Cultural Logic of Late Capitalism*, Duke University, 1991.

Kegley, Charles W. and Eugene R. Wittkopf. *World Politics: Trend and Transformation*, St. Martin's Press, Boston, 2001.

Lenin, "Imperialism: the Highest State of Capitalism," in Robert C. Tucker ed. *The Lenin Anthology*, Norton, 1975, 204-275.
Litaer, Bernard. "From the Real Economy to the Speculative," *IFG News*, published by the International Forum on Globalization online at Third World Network.

Mishel, Lawrence. "Grading the Jobs and Growth Plan," Economic Policy Institute, November 3, 2003, www.epi.org/policy/grading_jobs_and_growth_plan, pdf

Mishel, Lawrence, Jared Bernstein, and Heather Boushey. *The State of Working America, 2002/2003*, Cornell University Press, 2003, 277-307.

Mishel, Lawrence, Jared Bernstein, and John Schmitt. *The State of Working America, 2000/2001*, Cornell University Press, 2001.

Mishel, Lawrence, Jared Bernstein, and John Schmitt, *The State of Working America, 1998-1999*, Cornell University Press, 1999, 119-218.

Reich, Robert. *The Work of Nations: Preparing Ourselves for 21$^{st}$ Century Capitalism*. Knopf, 1991.

Rowan, David. "UN Report Says One Billion Suffer Extreme Poverty," World Socialist Web Site, July 28, 2003, www.wsws.org/articles/2003/jul.2003/unp-j28_prn.shtml

The Editors, "What Recovery?" *Monthly Review*, April, 2003.

United Nations Department of Social and Economic Affairs, *The World Social Situation: The Inequality Predicament*, UN, New York, 2005.

# Chapter 3

GLOBALIZATION, NEOLIBERALISM AND WORKERS

(With David Cormier, Institute for Labor Studies & Research, West Virginia University)

Political commentators, journalists, and economists have been talking about globalization since the collapse of the Socialist Bloc. Some are excited about it; others are terrified. Some activists from the political left and right mobilize against it, yet others, both left and right of center celebrate its promise.

This chapter walks the reader through a discussion of globalization and the neo-liberal policies that made the phenomenon a reality. It relates global processes and policies to capitalism today. It then surveys how globalization has affected workers. The central theme of this chapter is that the pursuit of profit and capital accumulation, the driving forces of capitalism, shape the contemporary global political economy; that even though the elements of the era of globalization, and late capitalism, are unique to the 21$^{st}$ century, the basic character of the global capitalist system, which emerged in the fifteenth century, remains the same. Effective resistance strategies require an understanding of the basic elements of capitalism as a system and what is new about capitalism today.

*Globalization: A Definition and Some Questions*

Whether writers embrace it, denounce it, believe it is something new or not, they all see it as involving a qualitative increase in the number and size of interactions across national, sovereign, borders. The common assumption is that trade, investment, financial speculation, the spread of images of Michael Jordan or Bono and the growing presence of McDonalds or Kentucky Fried Chicken and Levi Strauss, constitute a new global reality. The movement of money and jobs and idolization of sports and music icons is creating a world that knows fewer and fewer territorial divisions. A world organized around more or less secure nation-states for hundreds of years has been replaced by a new global system. In addition, the bounded nation-states promoted the economic interests of their own ruling classes and corporate and investment houses to the exclusion of those in other countries. Some theorists argue that today the political and economic boundaries of nation-states have been significantly reduced. Metaphorically, the military fortress has been replaced by the internet.

Much of the discussion of globalization has involved elaborating on a variety of questions. Are there important agents stimulating these interactions? Why do these agents act the way they do in the world? Have there been particular public policies that have encouraged the increased frequency of interactions? Further, have there been significant historical events or conditions that have increased the likelihood of globalization, such as the collapse of the Soviet Union? What are the root causes of globalization: new technology, the internet, or the continual and advanced drive for profit in a world largely free of impediments?

*Agents of Globalization*

While debates about their role, positive or negative, continue, multinational corporations (MNCs or what are often called transnational corporations or TNCs) clearly are agents of globalization by virtue of their size, the scope of their activities, and their presence in production, distribution, and consumption in just about every country in the world. As was discussed in the last chapter, these corporations have become more concentrated (that is a small number of them control a greater share of global economic activity). Data indicates that half of the world's biggest economic agents are multinational corporations (the other half being nation-states). And about 250 such corporations control about a quarter to a third of all that is produced on the face of the globe.

International banks and investment houses have dramatically increased in size, global presence, and power in recent times. Lenin pointed out in his famous essay *Imperialism: The Highest Stage of Capitalism* that banks, which in the 19th century had served as accountants for manufacturing capital, had become independent and powerful economic actors in the large capitalist countries. Banking capital, he said, had become integrated with industrial capital, thus creating a new version of capitalism, finance capital.

Lenin could not have foreseen the magnitude of the role of finance capital, which is a critical feature of the era of globalization. Banks and investment houses oversee the transfer of trillions of dollars of investment across the globe and fund the huge debt incurred by poor countries over the last thirty years. They manage the global speculation of capital that has become a staple of the current era, buying and selling currencies, stocks and bonds, properties, and in general paper with value. The radical shift in the magnitude of economic exchanges from those relating to trade in commodities to trade in paper is managed by these institutions.

Alexander pointed out that the global capital market volume increased from $1.5 trillion a day in 1990 to about $4 trillion in 1998. Further, at the time of writing, she estimated that the top twenty investment bankers in the world controlled 97 percent of the capital market business.

International organizations (IOs) increasingly have become the target of debate and popular mobilizations by those most critical of globalization. The Bretton Woods institutions-the International Monetary Fund (IMF) and the International Bank for Reconstruction and Development, or World Bank-were established at the end of World War II to manage international financial exchanges and to provide short and longer term assistance to war-devastated nations for economic reconstruction. A few years later, the General Agreements on Trade and Tariffs (GATT) was established as an organization of nations interested in trade liberalization. In 1995, the GATT system was transformed into the World Trade Organization (WTO) with over 130 nations as members. These three organizations were less than fully visible before the 1980s but have become the agents promoting a set of market-based economic policies, often referred to as "neo-liberal," that have led to the transformation of the economies of virtually every country in the world. By managing the dramatic increase of indebtedness since the 1970s, the IMF, the World Bank, and trade agreements (GATT, then WTO) increased the opportunity for international capitalist penetration of poor countries. With the collapse of Socialism, the possibilities increased enormously. As the IMF/World Bank/GATT-WTO institutions increased in influence over the global economy, the role of the United Nations, which gave voice to poor nations through the General Assembly, declined.

Although most would agree that MNCs, international financial institutions, and the IMF, World Bank, WTO triad are central actors in the globalization drama, disagreements abound concerning the role of nation-states in this transforming global process. However, it seems clear that some states provide the levers of power, military as well as economic, for the promotion of globalization, and other states, by virtue of their weakness, can serve only as enforcers of big state economic policies on the poor and oppressed.

The big state coalition most relevant to globalization is that of the so-called G7 countries. Even within that coalition of large capitalist countries the United States has asserted its role as global leader. This does not deny the significance of threats to that leadership from an integrating European system, for example, or an Asia dominated by Japan, or China (not a G7 member). One cannot separate the influence of global corporations and banks from the military power of the United States which in recent years has made war on Afghanistan and Iraq, has over 700 military bases in over 60 countries and has an FBI and CIA public and covert presence in many of those countries.

*Globalization: Trade, Production,*
*Investment, Speculation, and Debt*

The trading of commodities produced by one group of people to another is central to the construction of all civilizations. "Comparative advantage" was based on differential skills, resources, climates and the ability to produce some things better than others. Out of the growing specialization of society, trade became a staple of human interaction. In the capitalist era, commodities produced ever more efficiently required consumers in other communities or nations. If production was for profit, finding consumers was central to realizing that profit.

And so production of goods and, later, services became central to societies with growing populations and growing needs. A hallmark of capitalism was the bringing together of "free" labor to produce more and more products more efficiently. Since the dawn of capitalism, production has repeatedly been revolutionized in terms of use of technology, organization of work processes, distribution of units of production around the world, and mechanisms of worker control.

To promote production (usually at the lowest rates of workers' pay), increase access to markets, and stifle growing worker resistance, patterns of investment shifted significantly in the twentieth century. For example, during the formative years of the Cold War (1945 to the 1970s) investment increased more than trade. The largest global corporations began to produce larger shares of their products outside their home country. In the U.S. case, production of electronics, textiles, shoes, and other basic goods were shifted to low wage countries. Direct foreign investment became a primary source of capital accumulation and profit during the last half of the twentieth century.

The demise of the regulation of currency rates under the Bretton Woods system in the 1970s and the radical deregulation of economies in the 1980s stimulated an enormous increase in investment in intangible commodities: stocks, bonds, currencies, and various other forms of paper. These financial commodities exist mainly as zeroes and ones in computers and can be transferred anywhere in the world with the click of a computer mouse. Thus, there emerged a "virtual economy," of instantaneous global transactions that began to dwarf the trade in goods and services. National boundaries were traversed in surprising new ways. Paradoxically, foreign investments in goods, services, and paper in the United States began to exceed U.S. investment overseas. A new global finance capital arose that dwarfed the finance capital that Lenin wrote about just 80 years ago.

Finally, finance capital, and globalization in general, was facilitated by the growth of a system of international indebtedness that assumed enormous proportions in the 1970s. Oil-poor countries committed to industrial development had to borrow ever larger amounts to buy the oil which had dramatically increased in cost, due to instability in the

Middle East and oil crisis. The end result was burgeoning debt that by 2000 exceeded $4 trillion. Most countries fell into what Cheryl Payer called in the 1970s "the debt trap." Countries could never pay back even the interest on the debt they owed so they had to "reschedule" their debt, that is borrow some more. The IMF and private bankers would approve new loans if debtor nations changed their economic policies. They were forced to reduce tariffs, cut government spending, and generally make their economies attractive to foreign investors. These policies were part of the now familiar program of policies called "neo-liberal."

*Neo-liberal Economic Policies and Globalization*

With the collapse of Socialism, what is called neo-liberal globalization has expanded dramatically. "Neo-liberal" refers to a set of economic policies that are derived from the vision of Adam Smith and David Ricardo. These policies include limiting state involvement in economic life; promoting "markets;" reducing impediments to the global penetration of each and every country by capitalism (particularly in production, investment, trade, and finance); and finally privatizing the provision of all goods and services needed to maintain human existence. Emphasis is placed on reducing public services to citizens, such as access to cheap transportation, food subsidies, sanitation, and cheap water; privatizing public institutions, such as selling publicly owned businesses to private investors; and promoting exports of cheaply produced goods to wealthy countries, including shifting agricultural production from goods produced for local markets to crops for foreign consumers. Since globalization refers to a process of dramatically increasing cross-national interactions, particularly in trade, production, cultural exchange, and communication, the neo-liberal policies and the interactions are closely related.

Neo-liberalism as an ideology influences public policy today in nearly every state, whether industrial-capitalist, post-Socialist, or post-colonial. Every powerful global institution--the World Bank, the International Monetary Fund, the World Trade Organization, and the association of rich states known as the G7 countries--promotes neo-liberal policies. The most powerful instrument that global institutions have used over the years to induce countries to embrace the neo-liberal policy agenda has been the debt system. As suggested earlier, countries began borrowing billions of dollars in the 1970s due to dramatic increases in the price of oil. Now the world's nations owe banks trillions of dollars. Each loan or each decision to reschedule a debt comes with demands for economic "reform." In other words, banks, multinational corporations, and wealthy capitalist states force governments and people to accept the neo-liberal medicine.

Advocates of neo-liberalism claim that the policies they recommend will, in the long run, entice foreign investors which will stimulate economic development, rising living standards, and political democratization. For neo-liberals, the expansion of capitalist penetration helps needy countries grow. To the extent that globalization increases interactions of all kinds across sovereign borders, economic development will occur. "Global celebrants" believe that neo-liberal globalization will bring humanity to a new level of social and economic well- being. Data presented above and referred to below indicate that this claim has not been realized. In fact, many of the material conditions of peoples' lives over the last thirty years have gotten worse, not improved.

*Neo-Liberal Globalization and the United States Drive for Hegemony*

The United States at the end of World War II was *the* hegemonic power; that is it had the capacity to dominate international affairs economically, militarily, and politically. The United States held three-fourths of the world's invested capital and two-thirds of its industrial capacity in 1945. It had a monopoly on atomic power and, later, maintained atomic, nuclear, and air superiority over its adversary, the Soviet Union.  It was able to dictate the establishment of a variety of international economic and political institutions that served U.S. interests including the IMF, the World Bank, and the GATT trading system. As the Socialist Bloc and radical nationalist regimes emerged, the U.S. constructed an alliance system, the North Atlantic Treaty Organization (NATO) to defend "the free world" from Communism. This context provided the opportunity for the U.S. to plant the seeds of a system of global trade, investment, production, and financial speculation that flowered and grew through the years. From the days of the Marshall Plan program, transferring $14 billion in "aid" to war torn Europe-providing the recipients used the dollars to purchase goods from the U.S., to the trade pacts of the 1990s, to the Central American Free Trade Agreement (CAFTA) in 2005, United States foreign policy has been shaped by the vision of a neo-liberal world order. Its achievement was only constrained by social movements throughout the world with alternative perspectives on economic policy, and competing power blocs.

During the "Golden Age" of U.S. hegemony (1945 to 1968), the United States produced goods at home and shipped them to other nations. This included massive amounts of military equipment sent to selected allied countries. Because of the large foreign assistance programs for Europe and Japan after World War II, these countries accumulated the dollars to buy U.S. goods. Growing U.S. foreign investment occurred in agriculture and extractive industries such as oil, copper, rubber, and bauxite, all materials vital to industrial development and military production. U.S. foreign policy pursued the "Open Door," working toward the elimination of barriers to economic penetration. Even given U.S. power, resistance to U.S. penetration grew among Socialist, nationalist, and newly independent post-colonial regimes. The Cold War was a byproduct of the contradictions between these competing economic visions.

As worldwide resistance to the global agenda grew, the United States developed an interventionist and military response to it (as well as government opposition to labor militancy at home). Domestically, anti-Communism was elevated to a national crusade, consumerism was promoted, and an accord between conservative sectors of organized labor and management was fashioned.

During this so-called Golden Age, corporate profits grew substantially, real wages rose, social and economic benefits to some workers grew, while women and minorities remained left out. In short, the United States constructed a post-war global order to achieve the neo-liberal vision. Its full realization was blocked by international and domestic forces but U.S. economic and military power grew despite resistance to it.

By the late 1960s, global conditions had changed. European and Japanese products began to compete with U.S. made commodities. Political opposition to established power spread at home and abroad. The debacle of U.S. foreign policy in Vietnam substantially weakened American prestige and power. The U.S., still an economic and military giant, was no longer the hegemonic actor in the world. Its position was challenged militarily, politically, and economically, by the Socialist Bloc, by revolutionary regimes, movements around the periphery of the capitalist world, and by capitalist friends of the United States who had now become major competitors.

The Bretton Woods system, the system of established exchange rates to regularize trade, collapsed in 1971. Faced with growing inflation and the weakening dollar, and, as a result, increased foreign demand for gold in exchange for the dollars Europeans and others were holding, President Nixon announced that the U.S. would no longer exchange foreign held dollars for gold and deflated the once unshakable dollar.

In the aftermath of these decisions, exchange rates were allowed to "float," i.e. the price of any country's currency would be determined by "market forces." Exchange rates would then change precipitously, with the currencies of weaker economies made more vulnerable to dramatic fluctuations. As data reviewed earlier suggest, financial speculation rose. Massive fortunes were made in the virtual economy. Floating exchange rates coupled with liberalized investment rules set the stage for financial crises such as the Mexican peso crisis of 1994 and the Asian financial crisis of 1997.

Meanwhile, European and Asian goods began to compare favorably with U.S. goods in style, quality, and price. In 1973, an Organization of Petroleum Exporting Countries (OPEC) oil embargo during the war between Israel, Egypt, and Syria drove up energy prices, making the operation of U.S. cars more costly. Increasingly foreign exports appeared in U.S. markets. Significant among these were Japanese autos, German machine tools, and clothing and electronics from Asia.

U.S. foreign investment increased, including the opening of production facilities such as auto plants, steel mills, and clothing factories in countries where desired markets were located and/or where labor was cheaper than in the U.S. Spurred by dramatic tax cuts for the rich in President Reagan's first term, significant investments shifted from manufacturing and service to financial speculation.

As a result, de-industrialization escalated at home. American corporate investors bought or built production facilities or contracted for assembly operations with foreign capitalists; in short, a substantial increase in the export of U.S. capital and ultimately the export of millions of high-wage manufacturing jobs occurred. Paradoxically, foreign manufacturing transplants began to open in the United States in selected industries, such as auto and computers.

Real wages for the average U.S. worker peaked in 1973. Subsequently, wages and incomes declined because of declining rates of profit, increased competition from imported goods, the growing mobility of capital worldwide, the loss of higher paying manufacturing jobs, and the rise of lower wage service jobs. Real wages did increase during the last three years of the Clinton administration but increases were reversed in the new century.

In addition to the attack on good-paying manufacturing jobs, the Reagan administration began a systematic assault on government programs that had their roots in the New Deal, the Fair Deal, and the Great Society. Neoconservatives launched a campaign to reverse 40 years of government programs that were designed to guarantee worker rights and provide health care, housing, transportation, education and retirement security. As government was cut back, except for military spending, economic elites successfully pressured each administration from 1980 on to cut taxes for the rich while reducing social programs. De-industrialization wiped out more unionized jobs, union density declined, and bargaining power of labor weakened. The power of the working class had been significantly weakened by the 21$^{st}$ century, perhaps to a degree not seen since the dawn of the 20$^{th}$ century.

At the same time in the Global South many countries were forced to borrow more money from international banks to pay for the rising cost of oil. Banks holding profits from oil revenues readily lent money to these countries. As suggested earlier, a debt spiral was launched in which many countries became entrapped, borrowing billions of dollars with limited means for ever repaying their debt. The pattern of incurring balance of payments deficits (importing more than exporting), being unable to repay the interest on old debt, and incurring more debt in order to stabilize their economies became a regular feature of the international financial landscape. Poor countries victimized by the "debt trap" became prime targets for neo-liberal economic reforms enforced by the financial community. *Therefore, debt became the lever by which the global political economy influenced the destiny of most nations, and the majority of humankind.*

The era of neo-liberal globalization was initiated in the Carter administration and fully flowered during the reign of Reagan and his successors. Faced with declining rates of profit, growing economic competition from allies, revolutionary ferment around the Global South, and continued but weakening resistance to penetration from the Socialist Bloc, Reagan initiated a campaign to reestablish U.S. global hegemony to reverse the declining profit rates. Embracing policies very different from the pump-priming via social programs of the 1940s and 1950s, the policies of the 1980s radically increased the national debt through massive tax cuts and the largest peace time escalation of the arms race in U.S. history. Huge infusions of money from the tax cuts were channeled into financial speculation instead of U.S. manufacturing.

The tax cuts and the arms build-up, created a qualitatively increased national debt. It required the U.S. to borrow hundreds of billions of dollars from foreign investors during the 1980s. Foreign investment in the U.S. soared. With de-industrialization the U.S. economy shifted from producing goods to providing services while huge quantities of goods produced overseas were imported. Negative trade balances which began in the 1970s continued to grow. By the mid-1990s, the U.S., in Greider's terms, had become the trader of last resort. Despite the enormous annual trade deficits the global economy relied ultimately on the U.S. ability to import the increased goods produced in poor countries.

Foreign policy was intimately connected to international economy. Reagan embarked on a global military program to undermine and overthrow regimes that did not support marketization. "Low intensity" wars, that is wars fought with US weapons and training but not its own troops, were fought in Nicaragua, Angola, Ethiopia, Cambodia, and Afghanistan. The Reagan Doctrine called for the rollback of international Communism, including any regime that had relations with the Soviet Union. U.S. massive military spending, perhaps purposefully, drove the Soviet Union to compete which ultimately bankrupted its regime.

In the 1990s, the neo-liberal agenda was encouraged by the United States in the Western Hemisphere with NAFTA, in Asia with the Asian-Pacific Economic Cooperation network, and in the former Socialist states via intense financial support for pro-capitalist leaders such as Boris Yeltsin, President of Russia. President Clinton declared that his foreign policy priority was creating "market democracies." To that end he engaged in diplomacy and war in the former Yugoslavia, maintained a regular bombing campaign over Iraq, and sought to control Latin American countries through his "war on drugs" in Colombia, managing economic change in Bolivia, military training throughout the continent, and promotion of a hemisphere-wide free trade agreement.

The collapse of the Cold War international system meant the end of resistance to neo-liberal globalization. Even the former Socialist states would be penetrated by global capital. The process of globalization, begun at the dawn of capitalism, had finally reached world-wide dimensions. Economic consolidation and military power had conjoined in a new world order in which opposition from nation-states had almost completely collapsed.

*Impacts of Neo-Liberal Globalization*

Capitalism by any kind of measure has become more concentrated than ever before in world history (as suggested in Chapter 2).

Literally a few hundred corporations dominate manufacturing, retail commerce, and finance. Today's capitalism features growing concentration of capital, the flight of investments from domestic to cheap labor venues overseas, the rise of financial speculation, the rise of Post-Fordism, the shift from government social programs to a burgeoning informal economy, and economic inequalities in income and wealth within countries and between them.

Reviewing data from Chapter 2, in the United States, wealth and income inequalities had been growing since the 1970s. Rates of poverty have either stayed constant or worsened somewhat over the last thirty years. A longitudinal examination of wealth, income, and real wages, suggests that the U.S. economy became increasingly unequal and during the period of neo-liberal globalization (from the late 1970s to today). The condition of the vast majority of Americans has either stayed the same or worsened. Neo-liberal globalization may not have been the root cause of the worsening conditions of working people but it surely has not helped them either.

Unfortunately, global data demonstrate a parallel and growing gap between rich and poor everywhere. As reported earlier, nearly half the people on the globe live on less than $2 a day, and about 1.7 billion people live on less than $1 a day. The UNDP reported that at the dawn of the new century of the 4.6 billion people living in developing countries, more than 850 million were illiterate, a billion lacked access to water, and 2.4 billion lacked access to basic sanitation. Nearly 325 million children were out of school and 11 million under age five died each year from preventable diseases.

In 1980, according to a 2001 report by Weller, Scott, and Hersh, median income in the richest countries (top 10 percent) was 77 times greater than the median income in the poorest (bottom 10 percent). By 1999 the gap had grown to 122 times. The numbers of poor had grown from 1987 to 1998. The world's poorest people lived on 72 cents a day in 1980 and 78 cents in 1999. They concluded that "...the empirical evidence suggests that reductions in poverty and income inequality remain elusive in most parts of the world, and, moreover, that greater integration of deregulated trade and capital flows over the last two decades has likely undermined efforts to raise living standards for the world's poor" (Weller, Scott, and Hersch, 1).

The International Labor Organization (1999) presented data on stagnation and regression of working class life in Latin America. Virtually no employment growth in the higher wage manufacturing sector occurred between 1990 and 1998 while 85 percent of the new jobs were in the informal sector (informal sector jobs were estimated to constitute 59 percent of non-farm jobs), involving tiny businesses, personal services, and illegal activities. Work in the informal sector was low paid, had no labor protections or benefits. Of course, informal sector workers had no option of joining a labor union.

Meanwhile unemployment rates in the formal sector in Latin America grew in the decade from about 6 percent in 1990 to 8 percent in 1998. Unemployment among youth and women in most countries was double or triple the official unemployment rates. Economic desperation existed in the countryside as well as the cities. Massive rural to urban migration continued. In 1980, 66 percent of the labor force lived in cities and by 1998 the total reached 76 percent.

In addition, the ILO reported that workers' buying power in Latin America dropped. A 1980 minimum wage salary could purchase 27 percent more than a 1998 minimum wage salary. The average income of informal sector workers declined by one percent in the 1990s. In a press release, the ILO indicated that "...while overall poverty levels remained constant or decreased in most countries due to lower inflation and higher output growth, impoverished families continue to suffer disproportionately from the paucity of income opportunities and growing deterioration in the quality of employment (*ILO Press Releases*, 823/99,2).

In a *New York Times* article about conditions in Latin America, Larry Rohter wrote: "Almost without exception, economic growth in the region has either slowed or stalled altogether. Unemployment, crime and social violence are growing, as is popular frustration with a nominally democratic political system that has left many of the

350 million people in South America feeling that they are trapped in an endless cycle of stagnation, corruption, and incompetent rule" (April 13, 2002,1).

Finally, trade, one measure of globalization and the spread of the neo-liberal policy agenda, is celebrated by supporters of "free trade" as a vehicle to overcome income and wealth inequality and to lift workers from poverty and misery. In a series of impact assessments prepared by Economic Policy Institute researchers, EPI concludes that NAFTA has been a failure. Between 1994 and 2000, 766,000 U.S. jobs were lost due to NAFTA (Scott). The consequences of such a quantity of jobs lost to lower wage Mexico have included a continuing shift from higher wage manufacturing jobs to low wage service jobs, declining  real wages in the mid-1990s and since the beginning of the 21$^{st}$ century, and declining union effectiveness due to reduced membership and continuous threats to move production and service to Mexico.

Paradoxically, the researchers found that Mexico, now exporting more products to the U.S., has not benefited from the capital flight and increased trade. Declining U.S. production jobs meant growth in Mexican employment, primarily in deregulated areas such as the maquiladora zone along the U.S./Mexican border. These low wage jobs by U.S. and Canadian standards were not sufficiently robust to lift workers out of the category of the working poor. Further, with the concentration of new manufacturing in geographically isolated areas, the earnings of workers did not significantly infuse the national economy. Finally, 80 percent of the working age population of Mexico did not benefit from the new jobs, experiencing stagnating or declining wages.

The EPI reported that while Canada had experienced increased investment and trade since NAFTA, per capita income there had declined and income inequality had risen. Full time employment had declined over the seven years and the basic social safety nets, including national health care, had deteriorated.

EPI concluded that the modest economic recovery experienced in the U.S. and the region in the late 1990s (and since reversed) was not fueled by the predicted increases in trade, job creation, and investment. Rather, they claimed, economic growth was stimulated by expanded domestic consumer credit, brisk buying by U.S. consumers, and financial speculation and growth in the stock market. EPI warned that the Canadian, Mexican and U.S economies depended on U.S. consumers spending more than they earned. "As the air seeps out of that bubble, the cost of those nations' reliance on the U.S. consumer market is becoming apparent." The economies of the NAFTA countries in the new century confirmed the EPI projection.

*Assessing Neo-Liberal Globalization*

Reviewing the theory and practice of neo-liberal globalization leads to several conclusions. First, globalization has not brought the happy dawn of a new era of bliss to humankind. Any clear-headed assessment of the evidence indicates that in many ways the vast majority of people are leading lives of desperation. Indeed, advances in science, technology, and in public policy have impacted positively on health, education, communication, and transportation. However, at the same time, for the vast majority of the globe income, wealth, and political inequality have grown and the absolute numbers of people living in poverty have stayed the same or worsened.

Second, there is a connection between the downhill slide of humankind in economic, political, cultural and social terms and global public policies. Not only has the neo-liberal policy agenda not worked, but it has exacerbated human misery.

Third, globalization and its impacts are inextricably bound to the historic drive for profit, the very life-blood of the capitalist mode of production. Capitalism is a system that requires growth to survive-investments, production, trade, consumption, and new investments.

Fourth, the full flowering of the process of globalization and its policy agenda, neo-liberalism, was directly related to the collapse of the Cold War international system. The demise of a bloc of states animated by a different vision of economic and social organization, the Socialist Bloc, meant the end to organized resistance to global capitalist penetration.

Fifth, this system of globalization and neo-liberalism, the latest phase of capitalism, has had negative consequences for workers in the capitalist core, in the United States for one, and in the periphery, in Mexico, for example.

Sixth, the process of accumulation spearheaded by the drive for profits encounters a fundamental contradiction. The capitalist system is built on the purchasing of labor power for a wage that does not, indeed cannot given the pressure for profits, equal the value of products produced. Therefore, overproduction and underconsumption are recurring features of the system. Under the conditions of overproduction and under-consumption, rates of profit are subject to decline. With the pressures of competition, declining rates of profit force employers to cut wages or to move production to countries where labor costs are much reduced. Thus the process of globalization inevitably reduces the well-being of workers.

Seventh, economic crisis becomes political crisis when workers and their allies rise up in opposition to their circumstances. Progressive forces are, on the one hand, in disarray and, on the other hand, constructing new global movements against neo-liberal globalization, environmental devastation, war, and for worker and other human rights.

Points of contestation include struggles against the imposition of neo-liberalism by states (national campaigns) and global institutions (anti-globalization campaigns). There is no question that *both* states and transnational institutions are "enforcers" of the new economic policies, whether they use economic or military means. Local living wage campaigns or global campaigns for debt cancellation should be seen as part of the same struggle to overturn the late capitalist order and its international component, neo-liberal globalization.

*Bibliography*

Alexander, Nancy C. *Financial Times,* March 1, 1999.

Greider, William. *One World Ready or Not*, Simon and Schuster, 1997.

International Labor Organization. *ILO Press Release*, 1999, 823.

Payer, Cheryl. *The Debt Trap,* Monthly Review, 1975.

Rohter, Larry. "A Vicious Cycle: Failures and Instability," *New York Times*, April 13, 2002.

Scott, Robert E. "NAFTA's Hidden Costs," *Briefing Paper*, Economic Policy Institute, April, 2001, http://epinet.org

Weller, Christian E., Robert E. Scott, and Adam S. Hersh, "The Unreliable Record of Liberalized Trade," *Briefing Paper,* Economic Policy Institute, 2001, http://epinet.org

# Chapter 4

## MILITARY SPENDING AND ECONOMIC CRISIS

*Somehow this madness must cease. We must stop now. I speak for those whose land is being laid waste, whose homes are being destroyed, whose culture is being subverted. I speak for the poor of America who are paying the double price of smashed hopes and death and corruption in Vietnam. I speak as a citizen of the world, for the world as it stands aghast at the path we have taken (Rev. Dr. Martin Luther King, April 4, 1967).*

*War and Economic Justice*

In his dramatic condemnation of the United States war in Vietnam, Dr. King drew the connections between the victims of war in other countries and those within the United States. At the same time that U.S. firepower destroyed people and land in Vietnam, the costs of that war destroyed the hopes and dreams of poor and working people at home.

Also growing opposition to the Vietnam War challenged the national chauvinism created during the two World Wars and the "struggle against Communism" that followed. Vietnam era progressives, inspired by Dr. King, reexamined the connections between war spending and its negative consequences for the economy and the lives of the working class. The terrible costs of Vietnam and preparations for other Vietnams would subsequently impact on the debate about United States foreign policy in the Reagan era and would increasingly inform the growing opposition to George Bush's war on Iraq.

*The Historic Role of Military Spending*

Official U.S. government data from the early post-World War II years made it clear that the increased production to meet the demand for war material brought the US economy out of the Great

Depression and would bring significant changes in the way the economy worked. For example, 1943 industrial productivity was 2 ½ times greater than the average for the 1930s. U.S. trade increased by four times between the late 1930s and the early post-war period (Targ, 20). In addition, the impact of economic growth led a special Senate committee in 1946 to advise that wartime military contracts were given to a handful of the nation's largest corporations. As a result, they said, after the war there was emerging a qualitative increase in the power of a small number of corporations over the entire economy. One corporate CEO from a major recipient of wartime military contracts called for the continuation of a war economy during peace-time. This economy, he proposed, should make permanent the relationships between the corporate sector, research institutes and universities, and the military (Boyer and Morais).

Between 1945 and 1950, the anti-Communist crusade was used by capital, especially those corporations engaged in military production, to generate new demand for their products. The aerospace industry, in conjunction with the U.S. Air Force and some members of Congress, raised the specter of a war with the Soviet Union in 1948 to defend increased military appropriations.

Despite these growing pressures, fiscal conservatives in the Truman administration resisted significant increases in military spending until 1950. A critical Cold War document, National Security Council Document #68, was prepared and distributed inside the administration during that year by the Secretary of State. It called for unlimited military expenditures. And it suggested that every president should honor all military requests for funding before providing funds for any non-military expenditures. The military should be the number one priority of the federal government.

The Korean War was used to justify the proposals in NSC #68, which until the war started did not have majority support in the administration. Spending for that war and adoption of the recommendations in NSC #68 led to a fourfold increase in defense budgets in the 1950s compared to the late 1940s. The qualitative increase in military spending, on the Korean War and the arms race, helped stimulate U.S. economic recovery from a recession that had begun in 1949. The proposal for a war-time economy during peace-time has been a reality since the 1950s.

Even though military spending had risen from about $12 billion in the late 40s (in current dollars) to $40 billion in the 1950s, President Eisenhower was increasingly criticized for not spending enough on the military. During his second term advocates for significantly increased military spending for anti-guerrilla fighters, conventional forces, battlefield nuclear weapons, and more missiles and nuclear weapons increased their pressure on government. For them, reliance on the U.S. nuclear deterrent was not sufficient to stave off the Communist threat. What was needed, they said, was a "graduated deterrent," which, of course, required more money. Two prominent committees were formed, one by Eisenhower, to study defense needs. Their reports certified the needs for escalating military spending. In Eisenhower's last address as president, he warned of the growing and unwarranted influence of a "military-industrial complex" on American society.

Despite the outgoing president's warning, the authors of the two reports (Gaither and Rockefeller) representing significant sectors of the economic ruling class soon were in positions of influence in the new Kennedy Administration. Within his first six months in office, Kennedy had added $6 billion to military spending. He launched the program to train counter-insurgency forces, the Green Berets; he increased conventional force levels in Europe; and he expanded funding of nuclear weapons programs. Also, he authorized funds for military assistance programs and training anti-Communist military and vigilante forces in poor countries that U.S. officials said were "threatened by Communism." Finally, the Kennedy Administration increased research and development programs that would link academic researchers and major universities to the military.

Military spending increased by a third in the 1960s over the 1950s before the war in Vietnam escalated. By 1967, the U.S. was in a large land and air war in Asia. The costs of the war were threatening President Johnson's Great Society domestic programs. It was in the context of an escalating war in Vietnam and the threat to visionary domestic programs at home that Dr. King pointed out that education, health care, day care, legal aid, and other necessities for working class and poor Americans were being squandered as bullets flew, napalm was dropped, and bombs were detonated over literally millions of Asians. By the 1970s, military spending added to the "fiscal crisis of the state," as one economist labeled deepening economic stagnation (O'Connor).

Ronald Reagan entered office in 1981 in the midst of a deep recession (unemployment rates were above 7 percent) and during record levels of inflation (in excess of 10 percent). By the end of 1982, Reagan was able to fully rekindle the Cold War with the Soviet Union (dubbed the "evil empire") and launch a military program that cost more, in real dollars, than any time since 1945. Between 1981 and 1984, the increase in military expenditures of $140 billion was matched by an almost equal amount of program cuts in social services. Over the decade, the military budget (coupled with substantial tax cuts for the rich) stimulated an economic recovery in terms of rising GNP. But workers experienced declines in real wages and massive layoffs due to plant closings and capital flight.

During the Reagan era, anti-Communism as an ideology became popular again after years of skepticism brought on by the Vietnam war. It was paralleled by an ideological shift from the idea of positive government, government serving the human needs of its citizens, to negative government, government providing primarily military security and police protection while the private sector provides for all other needs. This latter worldview became the core assumption underlying neo-liberalism.

Between 1989 and 1991, the Socialist Bloc collapsed. Many Americans assumed that the end of the Cold War would mean significant reductions in grotesquely high military expenditures. The term "peace dividend" entered discussions of the federal budget. Military budgets, in current dollars, did decline in the 1990s, but not to the extent hoped for. Expenditures averaged over $260 billion during Clinton's second term. As he left office, DOD budgets were projected to increase beyond $300 billion by 2005. Military interventions in the 90s included the first Gulf War, troops in the former Yugoslavia, a war on Serbia in 1998, and decade long bombings of Iraq.

After 9/11, the current Bush Administration launched a military spending program to match the height of the Cold War. In response to the terrorism of 9/11, Bush attacked Afghanistan in 2001 for allegedly harboring Osama Bin Laden, the suspected leader of the international terrorist plot against the United States, and Iraq in 2003 purportedly because it was building "weapons of mass destruction" and was connected to the terrorists of 9/11. This time, U.S. foreign policy was driven by the "the war on terrorism."

In 2004, Congress authorized military expenditures in excess of $400 billion (including an additional $87 billion package for Iraqi occupation and reconstruction). Using arguments similar to those of NSC #68, President Bush claimed that military spending must be open-ended because of the war on terrorism. Even the "Communist" menace of the 1940s and 1950s had greater specificity as to place, people, ideology, government and duration of the struggle. The terrorist enemy was portrayed as the most elusive enemy in U.S. history. Terrorists were plotting against the United States in dozens of countries, potentially everywhere, and their allegiances were to a religious dogmatism, not any nation-state, that was committed to the destruction of the west. Academic ideologues referred to the threat as a "clash of civilizations." President Bush framed the struggle when he said that "they hate us because we are free."

*Direct Economic Effects of Military Spending*

In general, military spending in the new century has had a modest stimulating effect on the U.S. economy, but not quite as dramatic as in the 1950s, 1960s, or 1980s. Some analysts suggest that the Korean War military spending increases stimulated economic recovery from late 1940s recession, Kennedy era spending erased an Eisenhower recession of the late 1950s, and the dramatic increase in military spending in the Reagan era brought the U.S. economy out of the deep recession of the early 1980s.

War spending in the new century, it is estimated, has modestly stimulated the economy but not comparable to the above examples. Such spending today approaches 4 percent of GDP whereas during the 1980s it reached 7 percent and was about 11 percent in the 1950s and 1960s.

To be sure, Iraqi war costs include higher pay checks for troops, employment for some of the working poor and unemployed, and purchases of war supplies. But the primary economic growth derived from the new militarism may result more from shifting war strategies to the so-called Revolution in Military Affairs. RMA high tech weapons systems have meant allocation of resources for communications networks, robotic planes, smart bombs, and other instruments of automatic warfare. Cypher predicted that DOD investments in RMA weapons required construction of new production systems that would necessitate additional military expenditures of $100 billion. He concluded that the jump in military spending functions as an industrial policy for the information technology and communications industries, hard hit since the Silicon Valley economic bubble collapsed in the late 1990s.

So while the impacts of military spending may modestly impact on the economy as a whole, the information technology sector, and privileged private contractors for services such as Bechtel, Halliburton, and other corporations with access to the Bush Administration gain disproportionately from total expenditures. Kellogg Brown and Root (KBR), which is a subsidiary of Halliburton, has contracts estimated at a value of $7 billion with the Army Corps of Engineers and the Agency for International Development to repair the petroleum infrastructure of Iraq. After Dick Cheney was appointed Secretary of Defense in the administration of the first President Bush, KBR won, or was handed, contracts to study the privatization of army jobs and later received contracts to provide worldwide logistics for the Army Corps of Engineers. Since Dick Cheney left his Pentagon job to become CEO of Halliburton, and then became Vice President, the company had become the world's largest diversified energy services and construction company (Peterson).

In sum, military spending historically has provided at least modest stimulus for economic recovery and growth. Today the real financial beneficiaries of such spending are the specific production sectors, information technology and communications, that are asked to produce for the military; concretely those multinational corporations which receive huge government contracts for products and services. The latter contracts usually go to the companies whose high level personnel had  served in government and/or the military. The connections between government, military, and the corporate sector constitute what former President Eisenhower called the "military/industrial complex" and what Cypher more recently called "the iron triangle."

*Indirect Effects of Military Spending*

There are a variety of indirect effects of military spending on the economy as a whole and on the lives of most Americans. Military spending has always been capital intensive; that is the investment of dollars in military goods and services requires less labor power to produce than the investment of dollars in other sectors of the economy. Estimates of comparable dollar investments in the military, or highway construction, or public education find that fewer jobs are created by the former than the latter two categories of government expenditures. Even though more soldiers receive wages during a war and occupation, fewer workers are needed to produce the new high technology equipment that characterizes the new 21st century army. The Congressional Budget Office estimated in 2002 that $10 billion in military spending generates 40,000 fewer jobs than jobs generated from $10 billion spent on civilian programs (Gold).

Further, military spending requires the government to borrow money from private sources. The more money from private sources that is invested in government by buying treasury notes to cover deficits driven by military spending, the less money is available for investment in non-military sectors. Increased indebtedness due to growing military budgets may also drive up interest rates which dampen the ability of businesses to invest in their own expansion. In addition to "crowding out" investment dollars, expanding investments in the military reduce the resources of society that can be allocated for the production of goods and services that have a use value other than killing.

In addition to inadequate job creation and the crowding out of opportunities for non-military investments, military spending constitutes waste in that the resources that go into armies, navies, air forces, and weapons of human destruction cannot be put to constructive use. Two theorists with a particular analysis of military waste, Paul Sweezy and Paul Baran, claimed that capitalism always produces more surplus than it can absorb. Military waste is one of the few ways to overcome the tendency of the rate of surplus to rise under capitalism. These economists claimed that economic stagnation under capitalism was always probable as long as insufficient possibilities existed for waste. Historically military spending served an important role stabilizing the growth of capitalism by absorbing excess capital.

Perhaps the most important statement about the indirect negative consequences of military spending for society, the "drying up" of non-military government spending, was expressed by President Eisenhower who stated: "Every gun that is made, every warship launched, every rocket fired, signifies, in the final sense, a theft from those who hunger and are not fed, those who are cold and are not clothed" ( Wiesen Cook, 180).

*Indirect Effects of Military Spending Today*

When President Clinton left office his military planners projected a rise in DOD budgets from the $275 billion that had been reached in 1998 to $305 billion by the year 2005. President Bush's 2004 military budget (including the $87 billion he requested for the occupation and rebuilding of Iraq) totaled $470 billion, a total exceeding 4 percent of the GDP. Non-military spending declined as a percentage of the GDP from about 12.5 percent in 2000 to 12 percent in 2004. The National Priorities Project predicted a continual slide in non-defense spending. As the nation with the world's biggest military budget, the U.S. spent 30 cents of every tax dollar on the military and 19 cents on interest on debt incurred largely from military spending (National Priorities Project).

With military spending skyrocketing, approaching Vietnam era expenditures, government support for those desperately in need stagnates or declines. More than one in ten families live below officially designated poverty rates and 17 percent of all children live in poverty. Meanwhile, the National Priorities Project reports that government spending in support of Temporary Assistance to Needy Families (TANF) is less than 1 percent of the federal budget. Almost 11 percent of households in the country live with less than adequate food.

In addition, growing economic crisis for working people, costly higher education, decline in living wage jobs, reduced government programs, all force desperate working class youth to "volunteer" for the National Guard, Army Reserves or the regular army. Military service becomes one of the few sources of economic hope for youth in an economy of low wage and temporary jobs with no future.

U.S. Labor Against the War reported on data prepared by The Center for American Progress on what President Bush's request in early 2004 for an $87 billion supplemental authorization for the war on Iraq could have provided in non-military expenditures. Spent on domestic programs the $87 billion could have:

- more than paid for the total budget deficits of all 50 states.

- covered two years of unemployment benefits.

- paid 3.3 million workers who lost their jobs since 2001($26,363 for each worker)

- paid over seven times the cost for Title I funding for low income schools (funds cut by   one-third).

- paid for cuts in after school programs 87 times over.

- paid for special education programs nine times over current legislated amounts that were cut.

- paid for ten times what the government spends currently on environmental protection.

- paid eight times over for Pell Grant college scholarship programs.

- paid for the next three years of the President's Medicare drug program.

These and other data make the case clearly that military spending inevitably "crowds out" significant social programs and non-military expenditures at the national, state, and local levels. Only insiders can say whether key policymakers are making budget proposals to specifically take money from non-military programs to channel them to military ones. But, the evidence is overwhelming that the basic needs of growing percentages of the U.S. population are not being met and government resources that are designed to help meet basic needs, albeit modestly, are being reallocated to increasing military expenditures. The general point President Eisenhower made is still relevant today although the magnitude of the distortions of military spending for peoples' lives have grown to an extent unimagined in 1960.

*Political Effects of Military Spending*

Increased military spending affects the domestic political life of the country as well as United States foreign policy and international relations. As suggested, military spending is assuming a growing share of the federal budget while non-military programs are downsizing. Efforts to justify the spending draw upon the fears, to some degree legitimate, of Americans about their physical security. Recalling the days of NSC #68, the Bush Administration suggests that the "war on terrorism" has to be the number one priority of government, as fighting Communism was before.

Armed with the neo-liberal ideology, influential politicians and pundits suggest that the state should provide for security and nothing more while the market provides for all other human needs. The Bush administration is attempting to restructure government to destroy institutions and reverse policies based on the idea that government should serve the needs of its citizens socially and economically as well as providing security (the idea of positive government). Greider has argued that the Bush Administration has set its sights on returning government to the era of William McKinley before the demands of Progressives, Populists, and labor militants influenced the creation of the modern welfare state in the 20th century.

In addition to giving a significant impetus to the argument that the U.S. can no longer pay for social programs because of the exigencies of the war on terrorism, increased military expenditures give increasing political power to those sectors of the ruling class that represent the military, defense contractors, and their allies in Congress. The old notion of a "military/industrial complex" or an "iron triangle" takes on new meaning in the 21st century as increasing  government resources are placed in the hands of the managers of the war on terrorism.

During the height of the Cold War, President Eisenhower's warned of a possible "unwarranted influence" of the military/industrial complex on American society. Today, the war on terrorism has stimulated a renaissance of military values, national chauvinism, the institutionalization of military recruiting in public schools, the increased drive by administrators of universities to secure scarce research dollars to provide "homeland security" and a pervasive drive to "rally round the troops."

The connections between economic interest, military spending, a militarized political culture, demand for obedient support for United States foreign policy of necessity lead to the institutionalization of domestic repression. Reflections on the history of civil liberties in the United States makes it clear that rights and liberties embedded in founding documents are often under attack and usually the attack comes during times when political elites engage in foreign adventures and seek to stifle opposition to them. From the Alien and

Sedition Acts, to the jailing of anti-war activists during World War I, to the anti-Communist campaigns of the 1940s and 1950s, to the efforts to jail opponents of Central America policies in the 1980s, to the Patriot and Homeland Security Acts today, the connections between militarism and domestic repression are clear.

Finally, military spending must be assessed in the context of United States foreign policy. A program of global empire created and managed by "the last remaining superpower" has been proposed by key neo-conservatives in the Bush Administration. The drive for empire was clearly unveiled in the September, 2002 National Security Assessment released to Congress. It claimed that historically the United States promoted democratization and the development of market economies. It declared that the United States had a special role to play in creating market-based democracies around the world. It argued that the U.S. project was being threatened by "rogue" and "failing states," and, most importantly, diverse forms of international terrorism. In this context the United States, the report said, had to be equipped to respond to the forces of evil. The document argued therefore that the United States must shift from a policy of containment of enemies to a policy of "preemption." The United States, the document declared, reserves the right to attack nations and peoples when it is determined or surmised that enemies, governments or groups, were planning some assault on the U.S. And, despite the standard view that the U.S. goal has been to "contain" enemies, the NSS document claimed that the U.S. always had a policy of "preemption."

The Doctrine of Preemption has been bolstered by the construction of 40 to 50 new military bases in the Middle East, North Africa, and Asia (globally more than 700 bases in 60 countries). The wars on Afghanistan and Iraq were to be initial projects leading to a qualitative increase in the U.S. presence around the world: accessing and protecting energy resources; creating stable client regimes in troubled areas of the world; purging the last vestiges of the old Soviet Union's sphere of influence; and finally, opening the door for even further U.S. capital penetration (often in competition with capitalist giants in Europe and Asia and the rising potential economic power of China).

In the light of the new more expansive, military dominated foreign policy strategies, the domestic impacts and needs of military spending are intimately interconnected with the imperial goals of the Bush Administration. It is not necessary to discern which came first, economic interest at home or abroad. What is critical to understand is how military spending works and affects the domestic economic and political systems and, at the same time, promotes an imperial policy overseas.

*Military Spending and a Progressive Agenda*

This chapter argues that military spending has significant effects on the U. S. economy. (Ruth Sivard in *World Military and Social Expenditures* shows that global spending on the military exceeds spending for education and health). On the "positive" side, military spending historically, as today, has played a role in stimulating economic growth. During the height of the Cold War in the 1950s and 1960s, and in the Reagan period, military spending provided a kind of Keynesian boost to the economy. That is, such spending increased demand which lifted the economy out of recession. It should be noted, however, that such "military Keynesianism" was short-lived and aided some sectors of the society more than others. Currently, economists suggest, the stimulus of military spending is not as great.

The modest growth in the economy attributable to military spending is far outweighed by the negative consequences of such spending. It "crowds out" non-military spending. It leads to dramatic cuts in social spending at a time when more poor and working people are desperate for jobs, living wages, food, health care, shelter and other basic needs. (The lack of resources available for hurricane relief because of government priorities will be addressed in the concluding chapter.).

As to political effects, military spending gives life to rightwing ideologues who argue that government cannot afford non-military spending. It gives excessive power to military sectors of the ruling class. It gives material support to policies in pursuance of global empire. And it moves the U.S. further in the direction of a military state. Years ago, political scientists warned of the emergence of a "garrison state" in the United States.

In sum, military spending impacts on U.S. society in the following ways:

- provides huge rewards for select corporations that receive military contracts.

- puts excessive power in the hands of military interests: corporate, military, and political.

- threatens basic democratic rights and institutions.

- stimulates a U.S. political culture that celebrates war and violence.

- takes money away from the working class and disproportionately causes increased suffering among people of color and women

- and threatens the philosophy of positive government that has been inspired by the struggles to defend the interests of workers, African-Americans, Latinos, women, and others over the last half century.

*Bibliography*

Boyer, Richard and Herbert Morais. *Labor's Untold Story*, United Electrical, Radio, and Machine Workers, 1955.

Cypher, James. "The Iron Triangle: The New Military Buildup," *Dollars and Sense*, January/February, 2002.

Francis, David R. "War's Mixed Impact on a Reviving Economy,"*The Christian Science Monitor*, September 16, 2003, http://www.csmonitor.com/2003/0916.

Gold, David. "Fewer Jobs, Slower Growth: Military Spending Drains the Economy," *Dollars and Sense*, July-August, 2002.

Greider, William. "Rolling Back the 20th Century," *The Nation*, May 12, 2003.

King, Dr. Martin Luther Jr. "Beyond Vietnam," April 4, 1967, Stanford University, http://www.stanford.edu/group/King/publications/speeches/Beyond_Vietnam. pdf

National Priorities Project. "Where Do Your Tax Dollars Go?" April, 2005, www. Nationalpriorities.org

Peterson Laura. "Windfall of War: Kellogg, Brown, and Root (Halliburton)," The Center for Public Integrity, October, 2004, www.publicintegrity.org/wow/bio.aspr/act

Sivard, Ruth Leger. *World Military and Social Expenditures, 1996*, World Priorities, 1996.

Targ, Harry. *Strategy of an Empire in Decline*, MEP, 1987.

U.S. Labor Against the War. "What Can $87 Billion Buy? " 9/27/03, www.uslaboragainst war.org/article.php?id=3529

Wiesen Cook, Blanche. *The Declassified Eisenhower*, Penguin, 1984.

# Chapter 5

## PROGRESSIVE MOVEMENTS IN THE UNITED STATES

*What are Progressive Movements?*

Marx believed that all history was the history of class struggle. Class struggle was basic to history because all societies were class societies. Those classes that owned or controlled production, such as the factories or fields, gained disproportionately while those who worked as slaves, servants, or wage workers gained less.

Therefore, basic to the production and reproduction of life in class societies is inequality in wealth, power, and control which generates conflicts of interest. As history unfolds, these conflicts of interest stimulate mobilizations to demand change. The demands may be modest or fundamental. Sometimes mobilizations to create change, such as for a fair wage, escalate to demands for qualitative change, such as to destroy the economic and/or political system of inequality. Revolutionary movements are motivated by the belief that the basic institutions of society cause exploitation and oppression and therefore must be replaced by new institutions. Reformist movements strive to change some institutions and/or policies to alleviate human problems.

The Marxian assumption is that inequality in wealth, and therefore power, is basic to capitalist societies. As a consequence the economic organization of society fundamentally shapes all its institutions and relationships, including politics and culture. However, some inequalities, while parallel to and significant for the system of wealth and power, are derived from institutions, interests, and ideologies integral to but not necessarily derived from the economic system. Racism and sexism are vital to capitalist exploitation but have their roots in institutions and cultures preceding it. Racism is a system of control based on social constructions of what are called races; that is institutional and cultural categories that are used to define some peoples as superior and others inferior. Patriarchy is a system of power and control tied to gender. In addition to the economic structures of society, systems of racial oppression, and patriarchy, institutionalized forms of domination and subordination have existed based on religious beliefs or other characteristics of difference. In other words, the basic inequalities in wealth and power generated by class have been reinforced and replicated throughout societies in different economic, social, political, and cultural realms.

Given systems of inequality in wealth and power and the negative consequences of these inequalities, demands for change of varying kinds are essential features of societies. As suggested above, individuals and groups organize from time to time to create change: workers, people of color, women, or peoples of faith, for example. *Progressive movements are coalitions of groups who come together to bring about changes in policies and/or institutions to improve the lives of people and to reduce inequalities in wealth, power, and/or status.* They may come together to address issues of class, race, gender, religious intolerance, or specific problems such as abuse of the environment. More radical coalitions have a vision of changing several realms of economic, political, social, and cultural reality at once. Progressive movements are coalitions of groups who agree to work together because of some common purpose even if they do not share a particular understanding of history, economic and political structures, or a particular view of human possibilities. They realize that with numbers there is power and that a mass movement is needed to bring about some of the changes they desire.

*Kinds of Social Movements*

Political activism varies from country to country based on history and context. Some countries experience more mass mobilizations, street protests, frequent ouster of leaders, and violence than others. Also some countries have longer histories of leftwing political parties and Socialist movements than others. Despite significant variation in political histories, it is important to remember that social movements are basic to history and historical change.

Social movements differ as to vision as well as strategy and tactics. Movements have been created to solve specific problems in institutions or policies. These are *single issue movements*. Groups organize for living wage campaigns, to end particular wars, demand environmental protections, seek to protect women's right to choose and work on a whole host of other important issues. In societies such as the United States there are literally thousands of groups seeking changes that would improve humankind in some way and single-issue groups constitute the vast majority of this organized political activity.

Other movements are *multi-issue*, that is, they believe that issues of class, race, gender, the environment, and peace are interconnected and require a common approach to problem solving. Political parties committed to significant change, such as the Greens, serve this kind of purpose. Most mainstream parties, while they address a multiplicity of issues, do not have a vision or commitment to significant change.

Many movements are *reformist*, that is they promote modest but significant changes. Usually they work toward some policy change or institutional adjustment in the polity. Others organize with the goal of radically transforming economic and political institutions. Their vision is considerably more comprehensive drawing upon a systemic analysis of the underlying flaws in the economic and political order. Of course, Socialist movements foresee the overthrow of the capitalist system and its replacement by a humane Socialist society. These movements are r*evolutionary*.

Life is considerably more complicated than simple categorization schemes and social movements often consist of persons seeking change on individual issues as well as broader structural change. Also particular social movement activists may be motivated by a desire to reform while others may share more revolutionary visions of change and yet they are able to work together on common projects. But the fourfold categorization of social movements may help in examining and assessing past movements and at the same time clarifying what needs to be done to build a new progressive coalition for the 21st century.

*Single-Issue Reform Movements*

Throughout U.S. history, groups have formed to address specific changes in institutions and policies. Some, such as the environmental movement, have mobilized around single issues that have had long-term political and economic consequences. Most such groups have addressed individual policies of more limited impact such as supporting a clean water act or an endangered species act. Single-issue reform movements are often seen as part of the "pluralist" character of American politics, the standard social science rendition of how the political process works. Every citizen can participate in the policy process by joining a group. These groups organize around specific issues. For mainstream political scientists, single-issue reform groups are the heart and soul of U.S. democracy.

*Single-Issue Revolutionary Movements.*

Less common in U.S. history are single-issue movements that have a revolutionary agenda. Sometimes people mobilize around single issues without realizing the long-term consequences for economics and politics of their actions. Perhaps the Abolition Movement of the 19th century is the best example from U.S. history. What began as specific demands for institutional or policy change led to a growing mobilization that transformed society in significant ways.

*Multi-Issue Reform Movements*

These movements, less frequent, but very significant for U.S. history, involve a coming together around a variety of issues with a shared vision and purpose. For these reform movements, such as the Populists of the late 19th century, which sometimes include the mainstream political parties, institutional and policy changes are promoted with an eye towards rectifying social problems without radically changing the distributions of wealth and power. As the momentum for change escalates, significant economic and political changes might occur. Even though they are not revolutionary, the totality of the reforms add up to substantial economic and political changes. The New Deal reforms of the 1930s, discussed below, are an example.

*Multi-Issue Revolutionary Movements*

While having less of a presence in the United States than Europe, a Socialist left animated by a vision of radical transformation of the economy and the polity are relevant here. These movements have an analysis of the fundamental connection between capitalism and class, race, and gender that leads them to advocate a fundamental transformation of society. That is, the systems of capitalism, white supremacy, and patriarchy must be overturned and replaced with a new society based on humane visions of Socialism. At various times Socialist and Communist parties have had significant impact on U.S. politics. Paradoxically, their impacts have been to stimulate the creation of successful single- and multi-issue reform programs that have led to modest but valuable changes in institutions and policies.

*Generalizations About Single and Multiple Issue*
*Reform and Revolutionary Movements*

First, the practices of all social movements are shaped by their interaction with the forces that resist them. Oftentimes groups mobilize around an issue, encounter resistance, reexamine the systemic source of the resistance, then articulate demands for more fundamental change, and develop new strategies and tactics to achieve the new goals.

Second, resistance often leads to the development of a new understanding of the problem at hand. Single-issue campaigns, about environmental policy for example, might lead activists to the conclusion that opponents of reform represent corporate capitalists who oppose any restraint on their pursuit of profit.

Third, U.S. history is replete with examples of individuals and groups becoming "radicalized" by resistance to modest demands on single issues. As activists meet resistance, they begin to see that other groups with other agendas have experienced the same problems. Usually, confrontation with state power leads reform minded activists to develop a consciousness of "layers of causation" in reference to resistance to change. What begins as a campaign against recalcitrant politicians sometimes leads to a more systemic analysis of the economic underpinnings of support for the status quo.

Fourth, the character of the state reaction in the context in which the activism occurs  significantly affects the kind of activism that is advanced. Under certain circumstances, single-issue reform constitutes the most that can realistically be expected. At other times, a multiplicity of issues can be addressed in a comprehensive way and on rare occasions, analyses, vision, and tactics can take on a more revolutionary character.

Finally, "left" political activism should be based upon the historical possibilities that exist at any given time in history. Left participation in political activities of all sorts is important. The "left" contribution to building any progressive political movement should be to suggest an outlook based on a systematic theoretical understanding of society; for example, that human problems have a root cause or root causes; the variety of human problems are connected; and in the long run the solution to human problems require radical or revolutionary solutions.

*Cultural Fronts, the 1930s, and Progressive Movements*

Michael Denning has made an important theoretical contribution to the study of social movements in the United States. He introduced the notion of a "cultural front" to discussions about the 1930s and 1940s. He argued that in those decades, when masses of people were organized around and sympathetic to fundamental social change, networks of influences relating class struggle to politics and to culture seemed to be prevalent.

The primary political forces in the 1930s, the labor and Communist movements, indirectly influenced popular discourse and culture and how the vast majority of people viewed their times. Hundreds of thousands of workers were marching, striking, and sitting-in in factories to demand the right to form unions and thousands of them were affiliated and motivated by the Communist movements of the day. In daily newspapers, the saga of the Congress of Industrial Organizations (CIO) unfolded regularly. In many towns and cities workers not directly involved in organizing struggles were sympathetic to those workers who were. The newly emerging industrial unions, under the banner of the CIO, published newspapers, broadcast radio programs nationwide, and, in the case of Chicago, owned a radio station WCFL.

Communists, who had played a leading role in the early days of the CIO, had for years been involved in campaigns to demand relief for workers hit hard by the Depression, such as forming Unemployment Councils to demand welfare payments for the unemployed, supporting hunger marches, and agitating for an alternative to the kind of capitalism that brought the Great Depression. The Communists also played a leading role in challenging racism in the South: organizing against the charges of rape leveled against the young men of Scottsboro; demanding federal legislation against lynching; and organizing boycotts of businesses in cities like New York and Chicago which refused to hire African American workers.

Communists, Socialists, and peace activists organized opposition to European war in the 1930s. After the Soviet Union was attacked by Nazi Germany, the Communist Party joined with many Americans to support the war against fascism in Europe and later in Asia. Also Communists played a leading role in organizing the Abraham Lincoln Brigade, young American volunteers to fight against General Franco's fascist forces that attacked the beleaguered democratic regime in Spain.

In short, in the 1930s, class struggle was manifested in the nationwide drive to organize industrial workers in trade unions supported and encouraged by a Communist movement that had worked for years to organize industrial workers, a sector of the work force that had traditionally been excluded from unions. Also, the Communist left put the struggle against racism on the agenda. As masses mobilized, the unemployed, factory workers, and farmers, class struggle became a visible feature of public life. And workers,

Communists, Socialists, and pacifists, opposed war and fascism in Europe. Most of these currents were visible to Americans through the mass media. Denning suggests that union organizing was the driving force behind the visible presence of a progressive movement in the United States.

Arts and culture were inspired by the mass movements during the decade. Through the working class ballads of Woody Guthrie, the anti-colonial and anti-racist artistic politics of Paul Robeson, the proletarian novels of Jack Conroy and James T. Farrell, the artistic imagery of war and fascism in Picasso's Guernica, the worlds of work, politics, and struggle became the subjects of culture. Performers, as varied as Billie Holliday, Duke Ellington, Charlie Chaplin, and Marian Anderson, made artistic statements reflecting the progressive spirit, even though they were not affiliated with the CIO or the Communist Party. This is the point for Denning. The "cultural front" constituted a moment in history when organized movements, shaped by class struggle and Left parties, helped create a Left/center political coalition and inspired the creation of a broader progressive politics and culture.

The immediate political byproduct of the cultural front was the New Deal. Legislation was passed to give workers the right to form unions, to establish a minimum wage, to require some standards of health and safety at the work place, and to provide social security for specific categories of retirees. Unemployed people were put to work to build bridges, highways, and sidewalks, and to clean public parks. Others were paid to write and perform plays, to prepare histories of states, to photograph rural and urban life, and to document in writing the pain and suffering workers experienced during the Depression. While it is clear in retrospect that many African Americans did not receive adequate benefits from the New Deal, the seeds of the idea of "positive government" were planted.

The movements of the 1930s began with groups promoting single issues and evolved into campaigns for multiple issue reforms. In the background, but not insignificant to the epoch, were those Left organizations struggling for a revolutionary transformation of American, *while working with mass organizations to achieve multi-*

*issue reforms.* The Left/center coalition that developed over the decade constituted a progressive movement that significantly changed the economic, political, and cultural life of the country.

*The Cultural Front, the 1960s, and Progressive Movements*

The cultural front of the 1930s, including the changes in public policy brought by the epochal struggles of that time, still existed in weakened form in the 1960s. But it was a shell of its former self for a variety of reasons. Labor militancy was defused by CIO collaboration with capital during World War II. Labor/management agreements after the war replaced radical labor demands for control of the workplace for wage increases and benefits. Anti-Communism, the tool of repression, spread through the labor movement, schools and universities, government, and movies, radio, and television.

In sum, the shared values, beliefs, and politics of the 1930s became defined as subversive and un-American. And specifically, the Communist Party was hounded into isolation, as were many political and cultural performers and activists who had been sympathetic with it in years past. The network of connections between class struggle, politics, and culture were steadily dismantled and replaced by a "repressive cultural front" that defined progressive politics as an enemy force.

Manifestations of the cultural front of the 1930s, however, lingered on in the politics of the 1950s. Radical trade unionists continued the struggle for the right to organize and some, albeit a small fraction, in the labor movement continued to incorporate an anti-racist agenda in their work. In the South and across the nation, Tobacco Workers, Longshoremen, Packinghouse Workers, Mine, Mill, and Smelters continued the old CIO/Communist campaign; "Black, White, Unite and Fight." However, the mainstream of the labor movement, which became the AFL-CIO after a 1955 merger, significantly reduced its commitment to racial justice in the labor movement and the society at large.

In contrast, militant workers, committed religious leaders, and members of traditional civil rights organizations such as the

National Association for the Advancement of Colored People (NAACP), and most importantly rank and file African Americans launched a new civil rights movement that would shape the politics of the 1960s and 1970s. A new "cultural front" was initiated inadvertently by the Montgomery Bus Boycott of 1955. The working women and men who marched for miles to work instead of sitting in the back of city buses set off a nationwide explosion of forces: people of color, and youth, anti-war, students' rights, women's rights, and environmental activists.

As in the 1930s, the explosion of the spirit of activism spread throughout the culture. The politics of protest became a daily feature of electronic and print news, the subject of debate in cafes, barber shops, and legislative bodies. Folk and rock music became infused with messages of racial and social justice and peace. Movies and television, so constrained by the lingering anti-Communism of the 1950s, reluctantly and cautiously followed the music industry.

Finally, a politics of single issues shifted to a multi-issue consciousness and some activists shifted from reformism to revolution in their thinking about social change. By the late 1960s, discourse involved whether change could be brought about "inside the system" or required going "outside the system." Words like, the "establishment," usually ill-defined, implied an analysis of society that entailed economic and political institutions.

Importantly, the "old left," those activists who experienced the cultural front of the 1930s and concretely who had been schooled in Marxist theory and Communist or Socialist politics, were seen by younger activists as less relevant to the activism of the 1960s than the 1930s. The very label of the new movement, a label coined by maverick sociologist C. Wright Mills, reflected the disjuncture between the prior movements and the emerging one. It was Mills who called for the creation of a "new left." For him, this "new left" would rise up out of the passions of youth for social justice, particularly youth in the universities. This conception of the new movement implied that the working class was not central to change. Rather, this class defended the status quo.

Despite the fatal flaw in the idea of a "new left," that is its anti-worker character, the civil rights struggle and the inspiration it provided for students and anti-war activists created a political and cultural atmosphere in the 1960s that resembled that of the 1930s. Dr. King, Malcolm X, the Student Nonviolent Coordinating Committee (SNCC), and the Black Panther Party inspired a struggle first for basic social and economic justice and later for revolutionary change to create a system ending exploitation, racism, and war.

The civil rights and Black Power movements and the 1960s cultural front had significant policy consequences. The Voting Rights Act of 1965 and affirmative action programs could not have been embraced by the Johnson Administration and the Congress if mass movements had not demanded social and economic change. The panoply of programs known as the Great Society, including day care , preschool education, legal aid, and the modest Medicare and Medicaid programs, were reformist byproducts of the ferment. Ironically, several governmental programs were having measurable impacts but lost resources and support because of the escalating quagmire in Vietnam.

The Poor People's Campaign of 1968 symbolized the hope and the defeat of the 1960s cultural front. Dr. Martin Luther King had come to the view by the late 1960s that poverty, exploitation, racism, and militarism were interconnected. His conclusions about the interconnectedness of these issues and the need to fundamentally transform society to overcome them required the mobilization of poor people, Black and white, and progressives to demand fundamental change. His PPC was to culminate in a massive mobilization of progressive forces in Washington D. C. in May, 1968.

The development of his consciousness was reflected in his 1967 speech at Riverside Church in New York, in which he linked the war in Vietnam to racism and poverty at home. In addition, his support for striking garbage workers in Memphis, Tennessee reflected his efforts to link the issues of class and race. After Memphis, he was to lead the nationwide PPC walk to Washington to construct Resurrection City. He was never to make the trip and the

Resurrection City that was constructed on the mall in Washington was torn down in short order after it was erected. His assassination may have been connected in some way to the threat that Black/white unity around class and race issues represented to the dominant order.

The mass movements continued but the concrete (and theoretical) anchor that the PPC would have provided was destroyed. Various left formations emerged, the Students for a Democratic Society (SDS) splintered, and state repression escalated. The Black Panther Party, which was providing hot breakfasts and free health care to people in poorer communities, became the target of counterintelligence programs (COINTEL). Panthers were killed, arrested, jailed on trumped up charges, and their influence in the Black communities declined. Students were killed at Jackson State and Kent State universities. Meanwhile, products of popular culture shifted from social justice themes to interpersonal liberation. Rebellion was channeled more and more into consumerism. The United States presence in Vietnam came to an end in 1975 and so did the 1960s cultural front.

*Progressive Politics After the Cultural Fronts*

The "sixties" connoted something special as did the "thirties" before it. As has been suggested here, mobilizations around class and race stimulated the reassertion of people's campaigns of all sorts. Politics in turn impacted on culture and culture on politics. In terms of a mass psychology a sense of hope flowered and grew. In the 1940s and 1950s and again in the 1970s and beyond, the cultural fronts disintegrated and despair, isolation, and individualism replaced community, solidarity, and activism.

Several forces facilitated the demise of "the 60s." First, state repression escalated. Assassinations, police violence, arrests, and incarceration of many Black and white activists reduced the ranks of the leadership of existing organizations. Second, the global economy experienced stagnation and crisis spurred by two oil shocks. In the United States unemployment and inflation together rose precipitously. Capital flight escalated such that literally millions of high paying industrial jobs were lost as thousands of plants closed.

The percentage of the work force in unions began its significant decline. In the terms of the day the "economy of abundance" was replaced by an "economy of scarcity." When Ronald Reagan came in office an active campaign to destroy the labor movement was put in place, as symbolized by the successful effort to destroy the Professional Air Traffic Controllers Organization (PATCO).

Third, a long simmering right wing backlash to the 30s and the 60s gained significant force, aided by an attractive leader, Ronald Reagan. During his first term, Reagan launched a program that is still active and successful in 2005 to destroy the vestiges of positive government. Also he used the war against Communism, the "evil empire," to rekindle national chauvinism and massive increases in military spending. New campaigns were started to repress Central American activists and groups defending civil rights. His followers created campaigns against woman's right to choose an abortion, against gun control, for school prayer, and for the teaching of creationism to mobilize conservatives and some religious fundamentalists. The use of so-called "social issues" was designed to build a mass base of support for an economic and political ruling class that was committed to shifting the distribution of wealth and income even more to themselves by destroying positive government programs.

The quantum shift to the right nationally could not have occurred without apocryphal changes in progressive politics. Single issue politics continued, in some cases with admirable successes. Women's and gay rights movements flourished. Anti-nuclear and Central American solidarity movements successfully mobilized millions of people in opposition to Reagan's foreign policy. But the "old left" was in disarray; that is those multi-issue groups committed to a Socialist political vision. As the former Soviet Union and the Eastern European Socialist states experienced crises of political legitimacy and economic stagnation, the image of revolutionary Socialism became more tarnished. Most Socialist states disintegrated between 1989 and 1991, leaving only a handful committed in name, if not in principle, to Socialism. New post-Marxist theoretical currents among the academic left "deconstructed" the historical "narratives" such that the history of any revolutionary ideal became suspect. Class and class struggle as empirically grounded theoretical concepts were dismissed. Class was replaced by identities-racial, gender, sexual preference, and ethnic-as the focus of political attention. The Marxian idea of linking exploitation, oppression, domination and subordination to the economic character of the society was rejected as an intellectual tool.

The end result of the transformation and deconstruction of progressive movements was a politics of atomization: issues, identities, discourses, discrete contexts replaced a theoretical and practical understanding of history and attempts to understand the continuities between the past and the present were rejected. The dismissal of the Socialist project in general became fashionable on the intellectual left. At the level of electoral politics, the leadership of the Democratic Party shifted from being a party of opposition to being a party of centrist collaboration. The argument of those who rose to influence in the 1980s and 1990s, in the camp of President Clinton, was that electoral victory required embracing a variant of the Reagan revolution in politics to appeal to the "center."

The end result of these two developments was that the intellectual left rejected the historical and conceptual tools that would give vision and purpose to the possibility of constructing a "new new left." In the electoral arena, the Democratic Party, the sometimes agent of reform, embraced a new role, rejecting contestation and adopting collaboration as a political strategy. Meanwhile more wealth shifted to the top 1 percent of the population, real incomes declined for most workers, and the economic, political, and cultural manifestations of racism and sexism resembled the period before the Great Society of the 1960s.

*Political Crisis in the 21st Century*

George Bush won two disputed elections in 2000 and 2004. He is the creation of the neo-conservative, religious fundamentalist, rightwing faction of the capitalist class. During his reign wealth has continued to shift to the rich, workers and the poor have become as vulnerable as at any time since the Great Depression, and the United

States is attempting to reconstruct a worldwide capitalist empire that has been the dream of imperialists since the 1890s. This has meant unending wars in Afghanistan and Iraq, and threats of war against Syria, Iran and North Korea. Despite extraordinary demonstrations against war and racism and the rise of grassroots organizing, the movements are disjointed, single-issue, bereft of systemic analysis and vision. Of particular relevance is the weakness, to the point of near extinction, of the labor movement  The old anti-racist movement, whose heart was in civil rights and Black Power, does not evidence the solidarity of the past, nor the solidarity with other sectors of the progressive movement.

Clearly in the United States, and all across the globe, there is a need for a new mass movement which is multi-issue and reform/revolutionary. This new mass movement needs a class base. It must prioritize an anti-racist, anti-sexist agenda. It must be anti-imperialist. And the new progressive majority needs to ground itself in the public discourse and the culture of the majority of the people. The new progressive majority cannot replicate the prior periods of the cultural front but activists can learn from the strengths and weaknesses of the prior periods.

The times are right for a new progressive beginning. The vast majority of humankind lives in horrific material conditions. Massive mobilizations are spreading around the world concerning issues critical to people's lives. Numbers of passionately committed left intellectuals and cultural artists are growing. And, there is a history, even in the U.S., of socialist vision and practice.

*Bibliography*

Denning, Michael. *The Cultural Front*, Verso, 1996.

# Chapter 6

## WHERE DO WE GO FROM HERE?

### *The Contemporary Context*

This essay began with reference to so-called natural disasters such as Hurricane Katrina and then developed the argument that the contemporary system of U.S. and global capitalism constitutes an institutionalized economic, political, social and cultural disaster. This last chapter reviews the arguments made so far about late capitalism, neo-liberal globalization and militarism, their consequences, and historic efforts at social change. It then discusses images of change that should guide progressive politics in the short, medium, and the long run.

Chapter 2 borrowed from contemporary Marxist theorists who introduced the concept "late capitalism" to provide a short-hand way of referring to the latest developments in the U.S. and the global economy. Late capitalism referred to a qualitative increase in economic concentration and centralization; ever smaller numbers of huge corporations and banks that control larger shares of the economic well being of peoples all across the face of the globe. The proportion of profits derived from corporate manufacturing and service activities has declined as the share derivable from financial speculation has risen. A "virtual economy" has grown parallel to a "real economy' which produces goods and services vital to human well being.

Manufacturing, once the centerpiece of national economies, has become global while declining as a share of employment in most developed countries. Investment capital traverses the globe in the search for cheaper labor and natural resources. In addition, financial speculators seek short-term profit making opportunities, buying and selling stocks, bonds, currencies, and other pieces of paper in country after country. Increasingly, the life chances of workers everywhere are shaped by decisions made by CEOs from multinational enterprises and banks. States have increasingly become the enforcers of those decisions made by ruling classes at the apex of the capitalist system.

Combined with technological advances, work has shifted from high mass production and consumption to targeted production. Workers in the U.S. and elsewhere produce commodities for targeted markets. A large share of manufacturing labor has gone to the Global South where incorporation into the money economy has meant the destruction of economic survival in rural areas. Workers in poor countries become marginalized at the same time that jobs and good wages decline in core capitalist countries.

The paradoxical result of these processes described in chapters 2 and 3 is that extraordinary scientific and technological developments are occurring while the basic living conditions of the majority of humankind deteriorate. Central to this process of economic and technological development at one pole and growing misery at the other is the exploitation of the value of the labor of workers everywhere.

The prior chapters have suggested that the changing global political economy is fraught with contradictions. No contradiction is starker than the systemic capacity to produce goods and services, some to enhance life, at the same time that majorities find themselves less able to consume the products they produce. The growing poles of wealth and misery constitute an irreconcilable contradiction that has its roots in the very character of capitalism as an economic system.

Resistance has been central to all class societies. Marx saw the probability of political ferment, sometimes modest in goal and strategy and other times revolutionary, as integrally related to capitalist development. The great revolutions of the 20$^{th}$ century, in the former Soviet Union, China, Vietnam, and Cuba for example, and labor and socialist movements in western countries were intimately connected to the contradictory character of worldwide capitalist development.

Writers such as Lenin used the term "imperialism" to describe the global system of capitalist expansion and resistance. For him, the struggles between the poles of wealth and misery, and conflicts within the pole of wealth, would from time-to-time mean war and militarism. As Chapter 4 suggested, U.S. militarism and military spending were high priorities since the 1940s, both for profit and security. In total, Chapters 2, 3, and 4 provide an analysis of late capitalism, neo-liberal globalization, and militarism that can assist in the development of an understanding of the system that needs to be changed.

The historical examination of progressive movements in the United States suggested that often groups formed to address single issues in narrow and reformist ways. By implication a conceptual shift from single-issue to multi-issue politics, and, in the long run from reformist to revolutionary visions, would be necessary to address the global economic and political system of capitalism.

But, as suggested, the direction of mass movements must be guided by careful assessments of "the time of day," the context at a particular moment of history. The idea of a "cultural front" suggests the variety of political and cultural activities, visions, and programs that made "the 30s" and "the 60s" special periods in the history of progressive movements in the United States. In the two periods, class struggle and/or the struggle against racism provided the context for emerging mass movements of protest that led to profound political, social, and cultural networking. Progressive politics dominated the economic, moral, and cultural landscape of the country.  For our own day, constructing a new cultural front out of the massive mobilizations should be a central task of the left in addition to transforming single issue politics into multi-issue politics and reformist politics into revolutionary politics.

*A Progressive Agenda for Now:*
*Responding to Katrina*

The horrific tragedy of Hurricane Katrina, at a time in which the United States is embedded in a military quagmire in Iraq and in the context also of  efforts to radically reduce the role government should play in providing basic needs for people, has created an hour of decision for the United States. With New Orleans and surrounding areas near devastation and thousands of people displaced from their homes, their jobs, and their communities, governments can respond in one of two ways.

The pain and suffering of the affected peoples can be the occasion for a radical transformation of the affected areas into a "free market, neo-liberal zone." Public institutions can be replaced by private ones: schools, libraries, medical services can be completely privatized. Reconstruction of the affected areas can be transferred to the private sector, disempowering local, state, and federal government. And in the end only those residents would be allowed back to New Orleans and other devastated areas who meet the corporate master plan. Particularly, poor people, white and Black, would be excluded from the new New Orleans. This construction of a "free market, neo-liberal zone" is already under way.

An alternative approach to Gulf Coast reconstruction, the "positive government approach," would be to utilize the power and resources of government at all levels to rebuild the affected areas drawing upon the input, skills, and labor power of those displaced people who were the primary victims of the Hurricane. The emphasis would be on grassroots participation in deciding what should be rebuilt and what kind of community the residents want to construct. It would also draw upon the community for the primary labor to reconstruct buildings and roads and refigure schools, libraries, health clinics and other public institutions.

The centerpiece of such an approach would be a massive governmental expenditure, on the order of the Marshall Plan, which was a $14 billion economic assistance program for the rebuilding of Europe after World War II. It could utilize the example of the New Deal period as to labor: hiring workers from the affected communities to do the construction and service. This would accomplish the goals of reconstruction and putting people to work at livable wages.

Lastly, and most importantly, the vision of positive government underlying this plan would require active participation of those affected, rather than the "free market, neo-liberal" approach which would shift decision making power to the corporations and banks. This approach to recovery is virulently opposed by the economic and political ruling class at this time and has only limited support from Democratic "liberals" as well as Republican "neo-conservatives."

The struggle between "free market, neo-liberal" and "positive government" policies is under way as these words are being written. CEOs from hotel and other corporate elites with interests in one kind of New Orleans are already planning. Construction firms, such as Halliburton, have received huge contracts for rebuilding the city. And federal government officials have been suggesting that many of those displaced by the Hurricane in the city will not be returning to their communities. The initial flurry of promises of public assistance to the Gulf Coast region have disappeared.

On the other hand, progressive groups, particularly from the South, have been mobilizing to demand a positive government approach to reconstruction. One coalition in existence before the tragedy, Community Labor United (CLU), has been active in mobilizing groups and people. CLU is a coalition of religious activists, Greens, anti-racist activists, advocacy groups for families and children, artists, and trade unionists. CLU has created the People's Hurricane Relief Fund and Oversight Coalition.

An early CLU post-hurricane series of demands included the fundamental proposition that Gulf Coast residents must have "…the right to …to return to their homes and their communities and participate in reconstruction." Specific demands included: government funds for all families to be reunited; funds for relief be given to victims through a Victims Compensation Fund; representation by residents on all boards involved in reconstruction planning; public works jobs for displaced workers and residents at union wages; and finally, "transparency in the entire reconstruction process" so that citizens "know where all the monies are being spent and with whom they are being spent."

ACORN, a grassroots advocacy group for low income people, had its national office in New Orleans. It recognized that "low-income,

African-American and Latino families... are bearing the brunt of the suffering caused by Hurricane Katrina." Shortly after the disaster ACORN mobilized 35 town hall meetings to address the immediate needs of victims. Out of the meetings a series of proposals were adopted calling for survivor input into rebuilding, affordable housing, living wage jobs, and the reconstruction of public services. In mid-October, 2005, ACORN created the Katrina Survivors Association, a national effort to support the positive government approach to reconstruction.

The policy and action proposals reflected in the efforts of CLU and ACORN are not isolated responses to the needs of the people. The Center for Budget and Policy Priorities, in a document entitled "Bringing Katrina's Poorest Victims Home: Targeted Federal Assistance Will be Needed to Give Neediest Evacuees the Option to Return to Their Hometowns," challenges some of the early Bush proposals such as his "urban homesteading" plan. It concludes with the statement that "it is imperative not only that the basic needs of these families be met in the immediate aftermath of the storm, but also that those who wish to do so be able to return to their hometowns-and be able to locate in mixed-income neighborhoods that offer the employment and educational opportunities they will need to rebuild their lives and create adequate opportunities for their children" (Center for Budget and Policy Priorities, 14) .

*From Katrina to a National Progressive Agenda:*
*A New Economic Bill of Rights*

In Franklin Roosevelt's January, 1944 State of the Union address to Congress, he called for a "second Bill of Rights under which a new basis of security and prosperity can be established for all-regardless of station, race, or creed"(Rosenman, 40-42). This new "Economic Bill of Rights" included the right to a "useful and remunerative job;" adequate food, clothing and recreation; a "decent living;" freedom from "unfair competition and domination by monopolies at home or abroad;" a decent home; adequate medical care; access to a good education; and security from unemployment and old age for those not already covered by Social Security.

While the Economic Bill of Rights was never achieved in the United States, from the New Deal to the late 1970s elements of it were at least part of public discourse. Some policies, such as Social Security, addressed rights articulated by the President. The idea that government had some responsibility for the achievement of these rights was broadly accepted by the public and both mainstream political parties. Debate over public policy was framed within the assumptions of "positive government." With the electoral victory of Ronald Reagan in 1980 and the subsequent rise to power at all levels of government of rightwing politicians, government was redefined as the enemy of the rights of people.

In the wake of the rightwing counterrevolution in public policy, gaps between rich and poor grew and access to health care, education, housing and other priorities of the working people of the U.S. declined. The water and winds that washed away the mirage of economic and political stability in New Orleans uncovered enormous poverty and powerlessness. It became clear that America was still divided by class and race and that for the vast majority of people, the Economic Bill of Rights had not been guaranteed. In fact, the modest implementation of policies relevant to it was being reversed.

The meaning of these developments for 21$^{st}$ century progressives is clear. We need to launch a campaign to achieve a "New Economic Bill of Rights." Issues of well-paying jobs, adequate diet, affordable health care, educational opportunities, and comfortable housing are vital to working people in the United States *and* throughout the globe. The historical record of the last 30 years makes it clear that the satisfaction of human needs at home and abroad cannot be achieved by "the market." Government policies, the mobilization of societal resources, planning, and social commitment are required to reverse the declining human condition for a large percentage of the world's population. In short, the desperate circumstances of people in the Gulf Coast, in cities, towns, and rural areas in the U.S., elsewhere in the wealthy capitalist world and the Global South require the systematic mobilization of progressives on a scale even greater than in the 30s and the 60s.

*Late Capitalism,*
*Neo-liberal Globalization,*
*and Militarism are the Problems*

If the analyses in the preceding chapters are correct, there is an inverse relationship between capitalism, and its instrumentalities neo-liberal globalization and militarism, and the fulfillment of an Economic Bill of Rights. Competing political philosophies, personalities of politicians, interest groups, and political parties affect policies. Each of these factors needs to be addressed when pursuing progressive change. However, as progressives mobilize for change, they discover that below the surface of conventional politics are deep economic and political structures that shape the workings of societies. Political activists in the 1930s saw the connections between the Depression and the normal workings of capitalism. Even though Roosevelt was no radical, he campaigned in 1936 against the "economic royalists" who were impeding jobs and justice. The Poor People's Campaign of 1968 reflected Dr. King's recognition of the centrality of the economy for social justice. That campaign was designed to lead the movements of the day in the direction of class struggle

At some point in human history, fundamental structural change is required to improve the lot of humankind. And this means transforming the global economy from one based on private accumulation in a "marketplace" to one based on social need and planning. The first priority for the formation of a progressive community is the development of an agenda to address the multiplicity of people's immediate needs but as struggles around them develop, the underlying causes of problems become more clear. Reformist programs, of necessity, become more comprehensive. Links between domestic and global economic and political forces are uncovered. People see the connections between capitalism, war, and environmental deterioration. And clarity develops about the ways in which class exploitation, racial injustice, and gender discrimination develop together and serve the needs of profit. Ultimately the economic sub-structure becomes the subject of debate and action. Multi-issue reformism at some point is transformed into revolutionary ferment. This process occurs over a very long time. The project for progressives today and tomorrow is to build a community of activists who share a concern for people's lives and see the need to achieve a basic New Economic Bill of Rights for all people. Out of this struggle will emerge a passion to create a broader program of action to create a humane and democratic socialism. This is the long-term project.

*Bibliography*

ACORN. "ACORN's Work in the Wake of Katrina," November. 2005, www.Acorn.org

Fischer, Will and Barbara Sard. "Bringing Katrina's Poorest Victims Home," Center on Budget and Policy Priorities, November 3, 2005, www. cbpp.org

Rosenman, Samuel, ed. *The Public Papers & Addresses of Franklin D. Roosevelt*, Vol. XIII, Harper, 1950, 40-42.

The People's Hurricane Relief Fund and Oversight Coalition. "PHRF Demands," Community Labor United, November 4, 2005, http://cluline.live.radicaldesigns.org/page_id=52

# INDEX

Profit, 7, 13, 14, 18, 25, 26, 35, 36, 38, 39, 42, 44, 45, 50, 51, 72, 82, 84, 89

Progressive, 3, 25, 30, 32, 53, 70-77, 79, 80, 81, 82, 84, 86, 88, 89

Progun, 29

Proletarian, 23, 28, 74

# R

Race, 8, 28, 32, 45, 55, 68, 69, 70, 71, 76, 78, 87, 88, 89

Racism, 3, 11, 24, 31, 73, 74, 77, 78, 80, 81, 84

Radical, 15, 22, 30, 37, 39, 41, 69, 71-75, 85, 89

Reagan, 27, 44, 45, 46, 53, 56, 57, 65, 79, 80, 88

Recession, 22, 55, 56, 57, 65

Reconstruction, 37, 85

Reform, 14, 41, 45, 68, 70, 71, 72, 75, 76, 80, 81, 89

Resurrection, 78

Revolution, 11, 17, 39, 43, 45, 70, 71, 72, 73, 75, 76, 77, 79, 80, 83, 84, 90

Ricardo, 40

Rightwing, 28, 31, 65, 80, 88

Riverside, 78

RMA, 58

Roads, 85

Robert, 23, 33, 34, 52

Robeson, 2, 74

Robotic, 58

Rockefeller, 55

Rohter, 49, 52

Roosevelt, 87, 89, 90

Rosenman, 87, 90

# S

Schmitt, 21, 33, 34

Schuster, 33, 52

Science, 9, 11, 26, 27, 28, 50, 66, 71, 83

Scottsboro, 73

Sharpe, 33

Smith, 13, 40

SNCC, 77

Socialism, 3, 11, 31, 34, 35, 38, 40, 41, 42, 43, 45, 46, 51, 56, 69, 70, 71, 74, 77, 79, 80, 81

Stanford, 67

Superpower, 9, 29, 64

Superstructure, 8

Sweatshops, 18

Sweezy, 60

Syria, 43, 81

# T

Terrorism, 57

Theory, 11, 15, 17, 32, 36, 60, 73, 78, 80, 82

Troops, 6, 46, 57, 58, 63

Truman, 54

Tucker, 33

# U

UN, 8, 10, 21, 34

Underconsumption, 26, 27, 28, 51

Underdevelopment, 10, 20

Unions, 24, 25, 28, 32, 36, 41, 45, 46, 54, 56, 64, 73, 74, 75, 76, 79, 83, 86, 87

# V

Verso, 33, 81

Vietnam, 43, 53, 55, 56, 61, 67, 77, 78, 83

Virginia, 5, 35

Vote, 31, 77

Vouchers, 31

# W

Wages, 9, 18, 21, 22, 23, 24, 28, 42, 44, 47, 49, 51, 56, 59, 65, 83, 85, 86

Walmart, 16, 18

War, 3, 7, 11, 29, 30, 31, 37, 38, 42, 43, 46, 51, 53, 54, 55, 56, 57, 58, 59, 61, 62, 63, 64, 66, 67, 69, 74, 75, 77, 78, 79, 81, 84, 89

Washington, 78

WCFL, 73

Wealth, 7-10, 12-14, 16, 18, 19, 20, 22, 25, 29, 40, 41, 47, 49, 50, 68, 69, 71, 79, 80, 83, 84, 88

Weapons, 46, 55, 57, 58, 60

Weller, 47, 52

West, 5, 35
Western, 25, 46
Whites, 22
Wittkopf, 16, 33
Women, 7, 11, 21, 22, 24, 28, 30,
31, 42, 48, 66, 69, 76, 79
Woods, 27, 37, 39, 43
Workers, 11-19, 21-26, 28, 32, 35,
39, 42, 48, 49, 51, 56, 59, 61,
66-69, 73, 74, 75, 76, 78, 80, 82,
83, 85, 86
Workplace, 17, 75
Wright, 77

WTO, 37, 38

# Y

Yeltsin, 46
Yugoslavia, 46, 57

# Z

Znet, 10